123 Game Recipes

(123 Game Recipes - Volume 1)

Wendy Beran

Copyright: Published in the United States by Wendy Beran/ © WENDY BERAN

Published on December, 07 2020

All rights reserved. No part of this publication may be reproduced, stored in retrieval system, copied in any form or by any means, electronic, mechanical, photocopying, recording or otherwise transmitted without written permission from the publisher. Please do not participate in or encourage piracy of this material in any way. You must not circulate this book in any format. WENDY BERAN does not control or direct users' actions and is not responsible for the information or content shared, harm and/or actions of the book readers.

In accordance with the U.S. Copyright Act of 1976, the scanning, uploading and electronic sharing of any part of this book without the permission of the publisher constitute unlawful piracy and theft of the author's intellectual property. If you would like to use material from the book (other than just simply for reviewing the book), prior permission must be obtained by contacting the author at author@sauterecipes.com

Thank you for your support of the author's rights.

Content

123 AWESOME GAME RECIPES 5

1. (Very) Peppery Pate 5
2. 3 Sisters Stew 5
3. Anya Fernald's Chicken Hearts Cooked In Brown Butter 6
4. Apple Buckwheat Crumble Cake 6
5. Asian Inspired Braised Duck Legs 7
6. Asian Spiced Chicken Livers With Lemon Grass And Ramps 7
7. Bammy's Turkey Gravy 8
8. Basil Thai Noodles With Bison And Zucchini + Spicy Quick Pickled Cucumber 8
9. Best Turkey Omelet Ever 9
10. Bigos Polish Hunter's Stew 10
11. Bison Burgers On A Stick 10
12. Bison And Chicken Sausage Chili 11
13. Bleu Cheese Bison Burger 12
14. Braised Elk Short Ribs 12
15. Braised Gizzards 13
16. Buffalo Meatloaf 13
17. Buffalo Style Fried Chicken Livers 14
18. Carrot Potato Soup With Tiny Buffalo Meatballs 14
19. Chicken Fricassee 15
20. Chicken Galantine Or Pate De Campagne Asian Style 16
21. Chicken Liver Pate With Bourbon, Honey, And Sage 17
22. Chicken Liver Pâté 17
23. Chicken Liver Spread (née Pâté) 18
24. Chicken Livers With Jalapenos 18
25. Chicken Livers With Leeks And Kale 18
26. Chicken Or Rabbit In Creamy Dill & Garlic Sauce 19
27. Chili Aioli Buffalo Sliders 20
28. Cocoa Coriander Chili From Jenn De La Vega 20
29. Confit Of Duck Gizzards 21
30. Cooking With Tea! Old Fashion Roasted Chicken 22
31. Cornmeal Fried Frog Legs 23
32. Cow Brain 23
33. Crepinettes With Kale And Shallots 23
34. Crostini Toscana 24
35. Day After Casserole For A Hearty Breakfast 24
36. Dirty Rotten Roman Risotto 25
37. Double Cut Wild Caught Venison Chops With Plum And Guajillo Chile BBQ Sauce 25
38. Duck Bacon Topped Dates Stuffed W/Whiskey Infused Chipotle Sweet Potatoes ... 26
39. Duck Bolognese 27
40. Duck Confit, Pear, And Fennel Bites 27
41. Elk Pastrami 28
42. Everything Middle Eastern Seasoned Fried Alligator 28
43. Fab Chicken Liver Pâté 29
44. Farmer McGregor's Revenge 29
45. Fig Bindenfleisch Crumble With Crottin De Chavignol 30
46. Foie Gras Butter Pan Roasted Lamb Chops With Pistachio Fennel Dust 30
47. Foie Gras Au Gros Sel 31
48. Foie Gras, Roasted Figs With Raspberry Vinaigrette 31
49. Fried Rice With Duck Confit And Celeriac 32
50. Giblet Gravy 32
51. Goat Ragout With Figs & Rosemary Over Pappardelle 33
52. Grilled Quail With Sage And Pancetta 33
53. Grilled Wild Goose With A Fire Roasted Corn And Poblano Salsa 34
54. Guinea Fowl With Chestnut Stuffing (Faraona Ripiena Di Castagne) 35
55. Hare With Onions (Stifado) 36
56. Harvest Stew 36
57. Home Sweet Home Buffalo Chili 37
58. Indian Inspired Goat Rillette 37
59. Jacinta's Duck Rice Arroz De Pato Da Jacinta 38
60. Kashmiri Venison Burger 39
61. Lemon And Thyme Grouse Piccata 39
62. Life Path Paella 40
63. Liver Dumpling Meatballs In A Heavenly Broth 40
64. Loco Marinade 41
65. MOM'S TURKEY GIBLET GRAVY 41
66. Madras Goat Chili With Cucumber Raita .42
67. Madras Goat Curry 43

68. Maple Braised Rabbit And Carrots 43
69. Maple Glazed Magret De Canard (Duck Breasts) 44
70. My Brother's Pecan Crusted Venison 45
71. Old Fashioned Cornbread Stuffing 45
72. Ostrich Stuffed Peppers 45
73. Pan Fried Duck Livers On Wholemeal Toast 46
74. Paperino V Pierino; Duck Ragu And Pappardelle, The Thrilla In L'Aquila 46
75. Pappas Relenas (R.F.U.G.) Chubby Spud .. 48
76. Passion Fruit Muffins 48
77. Paul Virant's Make Ahead Roasted Turkey With Smothered Gravy 49
78. Pheasant Potpie 50
79. Pizza With Ducks Breast, Goat Cheese, Greens And Figs 51
80. Pomegranate Gastrique (Sauce) 52
81. Portmanteau'd Lamb Chops 52
82. RABBIT PAELLA 53
83. Rabbit Braised In Sour Cream And Horseradish Sauce 54
84. Rabbit Porchetta 54
85. Rabbit Sinatra Burgundy Style Rabbit, My Way (Warning: You May Also Make This With Chicken) 55
86. Rabbit Stew À La Rainier 56
87. Rabbit With White Wine And Rosemary .. 56
88. Rabbit À La Moutarde 57
89. Rhonda's Chicken Liver Pate 57
90. Roast Duck With Vegetables 58
91. Roast Gravy 58
92. Roasted Beets Paired With Duck Hearts .. 60
93. Roasted And Whipped Bone Marrow 60
94. Roman Style Oxtail Ragu 61
95. Rosemary Roasted Turkey 61
96. Salt And Pepper Kugel 62
97. Sautéed Frog Legs W/ Chubritza 62
98. Slow Cooker Venison Roast 63
99. Spare The Angst Classic Turkey Gravy 63
100. Spicy Plum Glazed Duck And Nectarine Salad 64
101. Spicy Venison Chili 65
102. Spicy Chipotle Bison Burger 65
103. Sweet And Sour Roast Goose With Autumn Squash And Cranberries 66
104. Tea Smoked Whole Duck With Plum Wine Sauce 66
105. Thanksgiving Turkey, Dressing, And Cranberry Monte Cristo 67
106. The Most Requested Pâté Ever 68
107. Tower Of Duck Gizzards Salad 68
108. Tripe With Chickpeas And Chorizo 69
109. Truffled Chicken Mousse 70
110. Turkey And Sage Biscuit Pot Pie (Gluten And Dairy Free) 71
111. Tuscan Chicken Liver Paté 72
112. Tuscan Inspired Bison Stew 72
113. Tuscan Liver Crostini Crostini Di Fegatini Toscani 73
114. Vanilla Spiced Duck Confit 73
115. Venison Jerky 74
116. Venison Steak And Eggs With Brown Butter Ramps 74
117. Venison And Haggis En Croute 75
118. Vietnamese Style Spicy Pig Ear Salad 75
119. Yoghurt Marinated Goat Steaks 76
120. Braised Rabbit Pappardelle With Mixed Spring Vegetables 76
121. Cake 78
122. Duck Magrets With Red Wine Cherries 78
123. Lapin À La Moutarde 79

INDEX 80
CONCLUSION 83

123 Awesome Game Recipes

***

1. (Very) Peppery Pate

Serving: Makes many servings | Prep: | Cook: | Ready in:

Ingredients

- For the chicken
- 8 ounces boneless skinless chicken thigh meat cut into 3/4 inch cubes
- 1 large garlic clove, very thinly sliced
- 1/2 teaspoon salt
- 1 teaspoon black pepper
- 2 pieces of salt pork about 1 inch square and 1/4 inch thick
- Olive oil to cover (5 -6 tablespoons)
- For the pate
- 1 pound chicken livers, cleaned and rinsed
- 4 tablespoons salted butter
- 2 tablespoons cognac
- 1/4 cup light cream
- 2 tablespoons drained green peppercorns in brine
- 2 tablespoons softened butter
- 1 teaspoon cracked black peppercorns (optional if you want very peppery pate)

Direction

- For the chicken
- Toss the chicken pieces with the salt, pepper and garlic and pack into a ramekin about 5 inches in diameter. Place the salt pork pieces on top and add enough olive oil to just cover.
- Cover tightly and roast at 275F for 1 to 1 1/4 hours. Set aside.
- For the pate
- In a large sauté pan, melt the butter and sauté the chicken liver for 6 or 7 minutes until barely pink inside. Take the pan off the heat and stir in the cognac. Cool the mixture a bit.
- In the bowl of a food processor, add the chicken, salt pork and garlic along with a tablespoon or 2 of the olive oil that the chicken was cooked in.
- Add the liver along with all the accumulated juices, the cream and butter and process until very smooth.
- Add the green peppercorns and the cracked black pepper if using and pulse until well combined. Taste and add more salt if you feel it's needed.
- Store covered in the fridge overnight. Bring to almost room temperature for serving with crackers, pita chips or little toasts.

2. 3 Sisters Stew

Serving: Serves 12 | Prep: | Cook: | Ready in:

Ingredients

- 1 pound Buffalo, ground or chunks (if you can't find buffalo use beef)
- 1 teaspoon garlic, minced (adjust to your taste)
- Oil, as needed
- 1 pound Butternut Squash, cubed
- 2 Onion, sweet, diced
- 2 Red Peppers, diced
- 2 cups Corn, fresh or frozen
- 2 cups Beef Stock
- 2 cups Tomato, diced
- 2 tablespoons Tomato paste
- 2 cans Pinto Beans*, drained
- 1 teaspoon Chili Powder
- 1 teaspoon Cumin
- 2 teaspoons Oregano
- Salt & Pepper to taste

Direction

- In a stock pot brown the meat with some oil, salt & pepper and garlic.
- Add the next four ingredients one at a time and sauté a couple minutes each to caramelize.
- Add stock bring to simmer.
- Add remaining ingredients.
- Simmer about 45 minutes.
- Feel free to adjust the seasoning to your taste. You can simmer longer and mash up some of the beans & squash to adjust its thickness.
- *Pinto or Tepary are traditional but you can use any type.

3. Anya Fernald's Chicken Hearts Cooked In Brown Butter

Serving: Serves 6 | Prep: | Cook: | Ready in:

Ingredients

- 2 tablespoons unsalted butter
- 1 1/2 cups chicken hearts
- Flaky salt, such as Maldon, for serving

Direction

- In a small cast-iron skillet over medium-high heat, melt the butter.
- When the milk solids are beginning to brown and the butter has a rich, nutty smell, add the chicken hearts and cook, tossing them around in the pan as if you're making popcorn, until browned on all sides, no more than 2 minutes.
- Remove from the pan with a slotted spoon, sprinkle with flaky salt, and serve immediately.

4. Apple Buckwheat Crumble Cake

Serving: Serves 12 | Prep: | Cook: | Ready in:

Ingredients

- For the cake:
- 2 cups pecans, (200gm)
- 1/2 cup butter or coconut oil
- 1/2 cup honey
- 4 large eggs
- 1/2 cup applesauce
- 2/3 cup buckwheat flour
- 1/2 cup cornstarch or arrowroot starch
- 2 teaspoons baking powder
- 1 tablespoon ground chia seeds
- 2 teaspoons cinnamon
- 2 cups grated apple, with peel, loosely packed
- For the crumble topping:
- 1/4 cup butter or coconut oil
- 1/4 cup sugar
- 1/2 cup buckwheat flour
- 1/4 cup quick oats
- 1/4 teaspoon cinnamon
- 2 tablespoons sesame seeds (optional)

Direction

- Preheat the oven to 350°F. Prepare a 9"x13" (22cmx30cm) pan by greasing it and lining it with parchment paper.
- In a food processor, grind the pecans until they are fine, but not starting to stick together into a butter.
- In the bowl of a mixer (or by hand) whip butter and honey until light and creamy. Beat in eggs, one at a time, until well incorporated, then add applesauce. The mixture will look curdly - that's okay.
- Add the buckwheat flour, arrowroot or cornstarch, baking powder, ground chia seeds, cinnamon and ground pecans. Mix well. Stir in the grated apple.
- Spread the batter into the prepared pan.
- Clean the bowl with a rubber spatula, but don't bother washing it because you can now make the topping in it. Mix all the ingredients for the crumble topping in the empty mixing bowl until crumbly. Spread the crumbles evenly over the batter in the pan.

- Bake for 45 minutes, or until a toothpick inserted in the middle comes out clean. Let cool slightly in pan, then cut into squares.
- Serve with a dollop of whip cream or ice cream. Keeps well at room temperature for several days.

5. Asian Inspired Braised Duck Legs

Serving: Serves 2 | Prep: | Cook: |Ready in:

Ingredients

- 2 Duck Legs
- 1 Onion
- 3 Garlic Cloves
- 2 inch piece Ginger
- 2 Dried Chillies ((fewer if you don't like heat, more if you really do)
- 2 teaspoons Chinese Five Spice
- 1 Bay Leaf
- 1.5 liters Chicken Stock
- 3 tablespoons Soy Sauce
- 3 tablespoons Hoisin
- 2 Pak Choi
- 1 tablespoon Toasted Sesame Oil

Direction

- Preheat your oven to 160°C/320°F.
- Begin by prepping the aromatics that will flavor your cooking liquor. Slice the onion, cut the ginger into matchsticks and cut both the garlic cloves and chilies in half lengthways. Because this is low and slow everything can be kept chunky and casual.
- Sauté the aromatics until soft before adding the bay leaf and Chinese five spice.
- Drop in the duck legs and cover with chicken stock and the other wet ingredients.
- Bring to the boil then simmer in the oven for 1 hour. Leave the lid on for the first 40 minutes, before leaving it uncovered for the last 20.
- Once your time is up remove the duck and place skin side down on a plate to cool. Meanwhile turn the oven up to 200°C/392°F.
- To crisp up the duck's skin – a key and very important step – brown the duck in the oven for about 10 minutes before finishing under the grill for a further 10. The duck should remain a reasonable distance from the grill – you don't want it to smoke and burn, but you do need it to render out some of the fat whilst crisping up the top layer.
- Whilst the duck finishes wash the pak choi and cut them in half lengthways.
- Heat the toasted sesame oil in a frying pan over a high-medium heat, and add the pak choi in when hot, cut side down.
- After about 3 mins, or when the cut side has started to turn golden, add a splash of water to the pan to steam the uncooked greens.
- Once the water has evaporated season with a little soy sauce and serve alongside the duck.
- Carbs of choice here would happily be rice or crispy garlicky potatoes.

6. Asian Spiced Chicken Livers With Lemon Grass And Ramps

Serving: Serves 6-8 | Prep: | Cook: |Ready in:

Ingredients

- • 1 pound freshest chicken livers (organic)
- • ½ cup good quality soy sauce
- • ½ cup water
- • ¼ cup dry sherry wine
- • 1 tablespoon sugar (I used honey)
- • ½ star anise
- • 1 small stick cinnamon (about 1-inch)
- • 1 ½ -inch slice fresh ginger (crushed)
- • 2 sprigs lemon grass (cut in 1-inch pieces, and crushed)
- • 1 bunch of Ramps or young garlic
- • ¼ teaspoon dry red pepper flakes
- 1 tablespoon vegetable oil

Direction

- Place livers in a pan, cover with water, and bring just to boiling; rinse and drain. In a sauce pan combine soy sauce, water, Sherry, sugar or honey, and oil. Add star anise, cinnamon, ginger, lemon grass or young garlic and red pepper flakes. Bring to a boil, reduce to simmer, add chicken levers, and reduce to simmer. Cover and cook on the lowest flame for 15 minutes.
- Remove from heat and cool. Chill for at least 1-2 hours. To serve, drain, discard all spices, and reduce the sauce until lightly thickened. Serve the sauce separately, or pour over the livers.

7. Bammy's Turkey Gravy

Serving: Serves 12 | Prep: | Cook: | Ready in:

Ingredients

- 2 quarts water
- turkey neck and giblets
- 1 white onion, chopped
- 4 celery stalks, leaves included, chopped
- 3 carrots, peeled, chopped
- 6 sprigs parsley
- 7 sprigs thyme
- 3 bay leaves
- 2 teaspoons chicken base (bouillon)
- pan rich with roasted turkey juices and bits
- 6-8 tablespoons flour, sifted
- Kosher salt and pepper

Direction

- For the stock, combine the first nine ingredients in a pot and let simmer for one hour, or more.
- Pass stock through a fine strainer and reserve the liquid. Trim off all usable meat from the neck. If desired, with a paring knife trim the giblets well. Cut neck meat and giblets into bite-sized pieces and add to stock. Discard all other vegetables and herbs. Cover and put in refrigerator; this step can be done a day ahead. You can use this stock and lots of butter to baste the turkey.
- To make the thickener, put the flour and two cups of the chilled turkey broth in a jar. With the lid on tight, shake vigorously until it is smooth with no lumps. (The stock cannot be hot, or else it will be lumpy.)
- To make the gravy, bring the turkey stock to a low simmer. When the turkey is done, remove it from the pan to rest and skim off most of the fat — but not the turkey juices! Place the roasting pan over a burner or two on the stovetop over medium heat.
- To incorporate the caramelized turkey bits and flavorful juices into the gravy, pour the thickener into the pan and bring to a simmer. Scrape up the bits from the bottom with a rubber spatula.
- While whisking, slowly add the stock to the pan. Whisk continuously until all is added — don't leave the stove, it is very important that you keep whisking! Return to boil and it will thicken to deeply flavored, silky gravy. Add salt and pepper to taste.

8. Basil Thai Noodles With Bison And Zucchini + Spicy Quick Pickled Cucumber

Serving: Serves 4 | Prep: | Cook: | Ready in:

Ingredients

- Basil Thai Noodles with Bison and Zucchini
- 1/2 pound wide rice noodles
- 1 tablespoon 2 teaspoons toasted sesame oil, divided
- 1 teaspoon sesame seeds
- 1 pound ground bison or grass fed ground beef (or tempeh if vegan)
- 1/4 teaspoon sea salt

- 1 medium yellow onion, sliced
- 1 inch piece ginger, peeled and minced
- 3 cloves garlic, minced
- 2 tablespoons coconut aminos, or 1 tablespoon soy sauce
- 2 tablespoons fish sauce
- 1 teaspoon coconut sugar
- 1 large carrot, thin matchstick cut or bias cut
- 1 large zucchini, medium matchstick cut
- 1 ounce Thai basil or regular basil (about 1 cup picked leaves), stemmed and left whole
- 2 limes, juiced
- 3 scallions, bias cut (reserve some of the green cuts for garnish)
- 1/2 cup roasted peanuts, to finish
- Spicy Quick Pickled Cucumber
- 1 cucumber, peeled and cut into quarter moons
- 1 clove garlic, smashed and peeled
- Pinch red pepper flakes
- 1/8 teaspoon sea salt
- 1 tablespoon unseasoned rice vinegar
- 1/2 teaspoon coconut sugar

Direction

- Basil Thai Noodles with Bison and Zucchini
- Cook wide rice noodles 9 minutes (may vary depending on the brand you buy- check package directions), and toss with toasted sesame oil and sesame seeds. Set aside.
- Sauté ground meat in oil in a large high sided skillet over high heat. Break it up as it cooks, but be careful not to agitate too much- you want to allow the meat to brown. Season with salt and remove from pan with a slotted spoon or spatula and add to noodles, trying to keep drippings in the pan.
- In the same pan you used to cook the meat, sauté onion, ginger, and garlic in drippings and remaining 2 teaspoons of toasted sesame oil over medium high heat, about 5 minutes. Deglaze pan with coconut aminos and fish sauce. Add carrot and zucchini and continue to cook, tossing frequently, about 5-8 minutes or until softened. Add vegetables to noodles, along with basil, lime juice and scallion. Toss

and serve. Garnish with reserved scallion and more sesame seeds or some roasted peanuts.
- Great with sesame roasted broccoli and spicy quick pickled cucumber (below).
- Spicy Quick Pickled Cucumber
- l ingredients, cover, and let marinate 20 minutes or overnight.

9. Best Turkey Omelet Ever

Serving: Serves 2 | Prep: | Cook: | Ready in:

Ingredients

- 3 eggs,, salt, pepper, garlic powder, milk
- 3 eggs
- 3 tablespoons milk
- 1 dash garlic powder
- 1 pinch salt
- 1 pinch pepper
- couple thin slices of turkey, couple thin slices of stuffing, 1 slice of baby swiss cheese
- 2 large thin slices of turkey
- 2 large thin slices of stuffing
- 1 slice of baby swiss cheese

Direction

- Crack three eggs and place in bowl, add 3 tablespoons of milk and a dash of garlic powder whisk together. While whisking eggs heat up pan (12 inch skillet) on low to med heat with two tablespoons of butter. Pour eggs into pan to start making omelet. Once eggs are setting lift sides of egg and tilt pan to slide uncooked eggs onto pan so the whole egg cooks. When the eggs are almost set
- Add thinly sliced turkey to one side of egg, place thinly sliced stuffing on top with a slice of baby Swiss cut in half and placed on top of stuffing. Flip the other side of egg mixture over these ingredients and remove from pan once omelet looks done. The cheese is usually a little melted. Sprinkle with salt and pepper

to taste. Cutting omelet in half will make two servings

10. Bigos Polish Hunter's Stew

Serving: Serves 4 - 6 | Prep: 0hours15mins | Cook: 1hours30mins | Ready in:

Ingredients

- 4 cups cups finely sliced Cabbage
- 4 cups cups Sauerkraut in brine (Not vinegar! Not wine!)
- 2 Onions
- 250 grams Organic Bacon
- 1 pound Artisanal Kielbasa Sausage, sliced into half moons.
- 1 Small Organic pork bavette/flank (optional)
- 1 teaspoon Caraway Seeds
- 6 Juniper Berries crushed
- 6 Allspice Berries crushed
- 4 Bay Leaves
- 1 handful Dried Porcini mushrooms (soaked in 1 cup boiled water)
- 1 cup Pitted Prunes
- 4 Apples (Mackintosh or a variety), peeled
- 750 milliliters Red Wine
- 2 Confit Duck Legs
- Freshly ground black pepper
- 1 tablespoon Tomato Paste (optional)

Direction

- Chop the bacon and brown in a Dutch oven. Remove and set aside. Pour off the fat. Add the chopped onion and sausage. Cook gently until onion is soft and sausage is browned. If using the pork bavette, slice against the grain and add to pot. Add the caraway, juniper, allspice and bay leaves.
- Meanwhile place the shredded cabbage in a large bowl and cover with boiling water to soften. Strain the cabbage and add to the pot. Cook five minutes.
- Add the sauerkraut (no need to rinse but squeeze out excess brine). Add prunes and 2 sliced apples. Add the bacon, wine and a generous grind of black pepper. Cover and cook over low heat for 45 min, stirring occasionally. Meanwhile shred the confit duck legs and add them to the mix. Cook 15 min longer. Taste and add seasoning if needed - usually the sauerkraut provides enough salt.
- Serve with good quality bread and butter. Smacznego!

11. Bison Burgers On A Stick

Serving: Serves 6 | Prep: | Cook: |Ready in:

Ingredients

- 1 pound ground bison
- 6 popsicle sticks or skewers
- 3 slices of bacon
- Shavings of your favorite cheese
- 1 beaten egg
- Oil for frying - I used peanut

Direction

- Be sure to have your condiments and garnishes (diced onion, pickles, relish, etc.) ready before you start frying. These are ready to eat the moment they're done.
- Divide the meat into 6 relatively equal pieces. Shape each into a rectangular shape about the width of a slice of bacon and about 3 inches long. Gently slide a stick or skewer into one end. Be sure it extends more than halfway through the length of the "burger". Lay them on a baking sheet lined with parchment and store in refrigerator while you get everything else ready.
- Cut the bacon strips into 3" sections.
- Use a peeler to shave off thin strips of your favorite cheese. Plan on 3 or 4 per burger. I've used Swiss, as well as crumbles of Gorgonzola.

- Lay out one sheet of puff pastry at a time on a sheet of parchment. Use a ruler as a guide to cut 6 pieces that are 5" by 3". Whisk up one egg.
- Begin heating your oil while you assemble the burgers.
- Remove the burgers from the refrigerator. Lay each one on a piece of puff pastry. Position them on one half such that when you fold the pastry over, the two edges will meet. Before folding, though, brush all edges of the pastry with the egg wash so that they'll stick together. Salt and pepper each burger. Next, lay a strip of bacon on top of each burger, followed by some shavings of cheese. Now fold the pastry over each burger, pressing a bit firmly so that all edges are sealed.
- When your oil reaches 375 degrees, you're ready to go. Unless your pan is huge, or you have a big deep fryer, plan to fry 2 or 3 at a time. Preheat an oven to 200 degrees to hold them as they get done, and line a baking sheet with paper towels. Carefully place 2 or 3 burgers at a time in the hot oil. Total frying time is 5 to 7 minutes, depending on how fast the pastry browns. At the half-way point, carefully turn each one over. When the pastry is beautifully browned, the burger inside will be about medium. Remove from the oil to the baking sheet and hold in the oven while you finish frying the rest.
- Yes, ma'am, two Bison Burgers on a Stick! Would you like ketchup, mayo, and mustard with those? Yes indeed, we have Grey Poupon! Some chopped onions? Of course! Maybe some diced tomatoes? Oh, lovely. Pickles, relish, or cornichons? Ah, very good choice! Enjoy the fair!

12. Bison And Chicken Sausage Chili

Serving: Serves 5 | Prep: | Cook: |Ready in:

Ingredients

- 1.5 pounds ground bison
- .5 pounds mild Italian chicken or turkey sausage (about 2 links)
- 1 tablespoon olive oil
- 1 medium onion, chopped
- 2 bell peppers (orange and/or yellow), roughly chopped
- 4 cloves garlic, minced
- 56 ounces (2-28 oz. cans) whole tomatoes with juice, roughly chopped
- 14.5 ounces (1 can) black beans, drained and rinsed
- 14.5 ounces (1 can) kidney beans, drained and rinsed
- 8 ounces tomato sauce
- 1 tablespoon tomato paste
- 1 tablespoon chili powder
- 2 teaspoons garlic powder
- 2 teaspoons onion powder
- 1 bay leaf
- salt and freshly ground black pepper, to taste

Direction

- Heat 1 T of olive oil over medium heat.
- Add chopped onion and cook for 5 minutes, until it is just becoming translucent.
- Add chopped bell peppers and cook for 2 minutes, then add garlic.
- When garlic becomes fragrant, but not brown (1 minute or so), add ground bison.
- Remove the chicken sausage from its casings and add the chicken as well. Discard casings.
- Add half of chili powder (about 2 tsp.) and pinches of salt and pepper. Stir frequently.
- When meat is no longer pink (8-10 minutes), reduce heat to low and add the chopped tomatoes with their juice.
- When incorporated, add the rinsed and drained beans.
- Add tomato sauce (you can use less, if you prefer, but the bison will soak it up) and the remaining seasonings: 2 tsp of chili powder, garlic and onion powders.
- Add bay leaf.

- Simmer chili on the stove, still on low heat, stirring occasionally, for 45-60 minutes. This allows the flavors to merry and the excess liquid to burn off.
- Remove the bay leaf and serve with light sour cream and a little cheddar cheese if you can't help yourself!

13. Bleu Cheese Bison Burger

Serving: Serves 4 | Prep: | Cook: | Ready in:

Ingredients

- 1 pound Ground bison
- 1 handful Herbed dry stuffing (I use gluten-free)
- 4 tablespoons Crumbled bleu cheese (maybe more!)
- 1 teaspoon Dried Italian herb seasoning
- Salt and freshly ground pepper

Direction

- Combine ground bison, stuffing, bleu cheese and herbs in a large bowl using your hands.
- Gently form into 4 to 6 patties.
- Generously salt and pepper both sides. Grill until the burgers have reached desired doneness.
- Serve on a beautiful piece of romaine lettuce topped with more crumbled blue cheese, tomato, and red onion. Enjoy!

14. Braised Elk Short Ribs

Serving: Serves 6 | Prep: | Cook: | Ready in:

Ingredients

- Red Wine Reduction
- 1 Bottle Red Wine
- 1 cup onion, diced
- 1 cup carrot, sliced
- 1 cup leeks, sliced
- 1 cup shallots, thinly sliced
- 1 cup mushrooms
- 3 sprigs thyme
- 3 sprigs parsley
- 2 bay leaves
- 1/2 teaspoon black peppercorns
- 3 cloves garlic, crushed, skin on
- Meat
- 2.5 pounds Elk Short Ribs
- Salt
- Freshly ground black pepper
- All-purpose flour
- Oil
- 1 cup Onion, diced
- 0.5 cups Carrot, sliced 0.5 inch thick
- 1.5 cups leeks, sliced 0.5 inch thick
- 2 Garlic cloves, smashed
- 2 sprigs Thyme
- 2 Bay leaves
- 5 cups Elk or beef stock

Direction

- Combine all the ingredients for the red wine reduction in a large pot. Bring to a simmer over medium-high heat and allow the liquid to reduce for 45mins.
- Season the short ribs with salt and pepper and lightly dust with flour. In a heavy skillet heat the oil over high heat until it reaches its smoke point. Sear the shorts ribs on both sides until golden brown and crusty.
- Set the short ribs aside. Add the vegetables, thyme and bay leaves to the reduced red wine reduction and toss. Now add the short ribs and the stock. Place the pot into a 325 degree oven for 2hours, until very tender.
- Transfer the meat to a heatproof container. Strain the braising liquid through a fine sieve and pour over the short ribs. Allow this to sit overnight.
- To serve, remove any solidified fat from the top of the liquid. Place the elk in a 400 degree oven with a little liquid until warmed through. Meanwhile reduce the remaining braising

liquid until it has a sauce consistency. Spoon the sauce over the shorts ribs before serving.

15. Braised Gizzards

Serving: Serves 6-8 | Prep: | Cook: | Ready in:

Ingredients

- 20 ounces chicken gizzards
- 1 yellow onion (small dice)
- 6 garlic cloves (minced)
- 2 cups white wine
- 5 cups chicken stock
- 1/2 cup frozen peas
- 1/2 teaspoon thyme
- olive oil
- salt & pepper

Direction

- Season the gizzards with salt and pepper. Get a wide pot with olive oil and sear the gizzards in batches until they are brown and have a nice sear.
- Remove the gizzards and add in the onion and garlic. Add more olive oil if necessary, cook until they are golden.
- Add the gizzards back to the pot and deglaze with the white wine. Make sure to scrape up all the brown bits from the bottom. Add the stock in and bring to a boil.
- Turn the flame as low as it will go and keep it on a very slow simmer. Cover 3/4 with a lid and cook for 4 1/2 to 5 hours. You may need to add water through the process if it reduces too quickly. You want the gizzards to be fork tender.
- Add the peas and thyme, cook for 10 minutes. Adjust the salt and pepper and enjoy!

16. Buffalo Meatloaf

Serving: Serves 4 (or 2 with leftovers) | Prep: | Cook: | Ready in:

Ingredients

- 8 ounces baby bella mushrooms, chopped
- 1 medium red onion, diced
- 2 tablespoons olive oil
- 1.5 tablespoons fresh thyme, chopped
- 1.5 tablespoons fresh sage, chopped
- 1/2 cup panko bread crumbs
- 1.5 pounds ground bison
- 1 cup tomato sauce
- 2 tablespoons tomato paste
- 1/4 cup milk
- 1 extra large egg
- 1 tablespoon crushed red pepper flakes
- 1/2 teaspoon salt
- 1/2 teaspoon pepper

Direction

- Preheat oven to 375 degrees.
- Heat olive oil in a medium pan. Sauté diced mushrooms and onions until onions are soft and mushrooms are browned, about 5 to 7 minutes. Turn off the heat and add chopped thyme and sage. Cool slightly.
- Combine cooled mushroom mixture, bread crumbs, 1/2 cup tomato sauce, 1 T. tomato paste, milk, egg, 1/2 T. crushed red pepper flakes, salt, and pepper.
- Mix buffalo with meatloaf base mixture. Mix until just combined. Form into a loaf on a sheet pan.
- Roast meatloaf in oven for 30 minutes.
- In the meantime, combine remaining 1/2 cup tomato sauce, 1 T. tomato paste, and 1/2 T. red pepper flakes. After the meatloaf has been baking for 30 minutes, pour tomato sauce evenly over top of loaf.
- Roast the meatloaf an additional 20 minutes. Remove from oven and let rest for 5 to 10 minutes.
- Slice, serve, and enjoy!

17. Buffalo Style Fried Chicken Livers

Serving: Serves 2 as an appetizer | Prep: | Cook: | Ready in:

Ingredients

- Buffalo-Style Fried Chicken Livers
- 4 ounces chicken livers
- 1 cup buttermilk, divided
- 1/2 cup all-purpose flour
- 1 teaspoon Kosher or sea salt
- 1/2 teaspoon hot Hungarian paprika
- 1/2 teaspoon Old Bay seasoning
- 1/4 teaspoon cayenne pepper
- 1/2 cup grapeseed or other neutral-flavored oil
- 1/4 cup unsalted butter
- 1/4 cup Sriracha or other hot pepper sauce
- for serving: celery and/or carrot sticks, blue cheese dressing or dip
- Blue Cheese Dressing
- 1 small clove of garlic
- 1 teaspoon coarse sea salt
- 1 tablespoon mayonnaise
- 1/4 cup crème fraiche
- 1 tablespoon buttermilk
- a splash of sherry vinegar
- 1/4 cup crumbled blue cheese
- Kosher or sea salt and freshly cracked black pepper, to taste

Direction

- Buffalo-Style Fried Chicken Livers
- Separate the chicken livers into two lobes, and trim and discard any sinewy bits or veins. Cut each lobe in half and set aside.
- Pour ½ cup of the buttermilk into a bowl. Add the chicken livers to the buttermilk and let soak for 5-10 minutes.
- Place the flour in a shallow dish and add the salt, paprika, Old Bay, and cayenne, stirring with a fork until the spices are evenly distributed. Remove the livers from the buttermilk and dredge them in the flour. Discard the buttermilk, wipe out the bowl and add the remaining ½ cup of buttermilk. Dip the livers in the buttermilk and dredge them a second time in the seasoned flour.
- Place the oil in a heavy-bottomed skillet and warm over medium heat until shimmering. Carefully add the livers a few at a time to the hot oil, cooking for a few minutes per side until they are golden brown and crispy. Remove the cooked livers to a paper towel-lined platter, and continue cooking in batches until all of the livers are fried. Note: you'll want to use a splatter shield over your pan, as the livers will pop and spatter. Also, if you're making a larger batch of these, you can hold the fried livers on a rack in a low oven to keep them warm until serving.
- While the livers are frying, melt the butter in a small saucepan. Whisk in the hot sauce until well incorporated. Just before serving, gently toss the fried livers in the butter and hot sauce mixture. Place the sauced livers on a plate or platter, and serve with celery and/or carrot sticks and your favorite blue cheese dressing or dip – and plenty of napkins.
- Blue Cheese Dressing
- Peel the garlic and sprinkle the salt over it. With the side of a knife, mash the salt and garlic to a paste and scrape into a small bowl.
- Add the mayonnaise, crème fraiche, buttermilk, and sherry vinegar to the bowl and whisk to combine.
- Stir in the blue cheese and season to taste with salt and pepper. Chill for 20-30 minutes before serving.

18. Carrot Potato Soup With Tiny Buffalo Meatballs

Serving: Serves about 4-6 | Prep: | Cook: | Ready in:

Ingredients

- Creamy Carrot Potato Soup
- 2 tablespoons extra virgin olive oil
- 1 pound carrots, peeled and diced
- 1 large onion, chopped
- 1 medium potato, scrubbed and chopped
- 3 garlic cloves, smashed
- 1 tablespoon tomato paste
- 1/2-1 teaspoons salt
- few grindings of black pepper
- 5 cups not too salty stock (vegetable, beef, chicken, duck...it's up to you)
- Tiny Buffalo Meatballs
- 1 pound ground buffalo meat
- 2 handfuls breadcrumbs (I use ground up seasoned whole wheat matzoh)
- 1 egg
- 1/2 cup grated Parmigiano-Reggiano cheese
- 3/4 teaspoon salt
- pinch of red pepper flakes

Direction

- Creamy Carrot Potato Soup
- In a large stockpot, heat the olive oil over medium high heat. Add the carrots, onions, potato, and garlic. Add the salt and pepper. Sauté for a few minutes and add the tomato paste and stir to coat. Add the stock of your choice, bring to a boil, lower heat to low, cover, and simmer for about 35 minutes. In two batches, blitz the soup until smooth and creamy (don't fill the blender up completely and blend with a towel placed over the hole in the cover to keep from spattering all over your kitchen). Return to stockpot and adjust for salt and pepper.
- Tiny Buffalo Meatballs
- Preheat oven to 350F. Mix the buffalo mixture together and form into little meatballs. Bake for 8-10 minutes. Put into the soup and serve.
- I also chopped up some kalamata olives and stirred them into the soup as I was serving it. They deepened to color of the soup and gave a welcome tang to it.

19. Chicken Fricassee

Serving: Serves 6 | Prep: | Cook: | Ready in:

Ingredients

- 1 1/4 pounds lean, first cut flanken (top rib) from a kosher butcher. This is similar to short rib, but cut across the bone. Trim any large pieces of fat and cut into bite-sized pieces. Leave some meat attached to each bone.
- 1/2 pound chicken gizzards, trimmed of any green or yellow skin and halved
- 2 1/2 pounds chicken wings, cut at the joints and tips reserved for another use, or the same amount of drumsticks (I like to remove the skin)
- Olive oil, for browning meat
- 1 container Pomi strained tomatoes (26.46-ounce box) or canned or jarred strained tomatoes of similar package size.
- 2 tablespoons sugar (I use natural cane sugar), plus more to taste
- 2 tablespoons freshly squeezed lemon juice, plus more to taste
- 1 teaspoon salt, plus more to taste
- a few grinds of pepper to taste
- about 12 ounces water
- Rice, for serving

Direction

- Season the meat, gizzards, and wings, with salt and pepper. Then add a slick of oil to the bottom of a large heavy pot and heat over medium-high. Then brown the flanken on both sides. Do not crowd the pan, even if it means doing the browning in a couple of batches. After each batch is finished, remove the pieces to a bowl and set aside.
- Heat olive oil in a skillet or frying pan, then brown the gizzards and set aside.
- Put the browned flanken back into the pot and add the browned gizzards. Add the strained tomatoes, sugar, lemon juice, salt, and pepper. Put the water into the Pomi box or other

- tomato container (so that you can get all of the tomato goodness) and swish it around a little, then add that as well. The liquid should cover the meat.
- Bring the liquid to a boil, then lower the heat to keep the contents at a steady simmer. Scrape up the bits that might have gotten stuck to the bottom of the pan during browning. Cover the pot, leaving the lid ajar. Simmer like this about an hour.
- Clean out the gizzard frying pan and brown the chicken wings until crispy. Set aside.
- After the first hour, taste the sauce and add sugar and/or lemon juice to balance the sweet/salty flavor to your liking. Taste for salt and pepper. Add the chicken wings and continue to simmer for about another hour with the pot lid ajar.
- After another hour, taste for salt, sugar, and lemon once again. If you have the time, let it simmer another half an hour.
- If possible, let cool and refrigerate overnight. The sauce gets better the next day and you can skim the fat off before reheating to serve. Delicious with rice.

20. Chicken Galantine Or Pate De Campagne Asian Style

Serving: Serves 8 to 10 | Prep: | Cook: |Ready in:

Ingredients

- • 2 tablespoons of each soy sauce, dry sherry, and Hoisin sauce
- • 2 teaspoons of each cornstarch and vegetable or canola oil
- • 1 teaspoons of each sesame oil and sugar
- • ½ teaspoon of freshly ground black pepper
- • 1 pound of each chicken breast and thighs, very carefully skinned, boned, and cut in bite-size pieces
- • 2 medium shallots or 1 onion, diced
- • 1 teaspoon of ground coriander or 1 tablespoon of fresh cilantro leaves
- • 2 tablespoons oil for the Terrine

Direction

- In a bowl, combine soy, sherry, Hoisin sauce, cornstarch, vegetable or canola oil, sesame oil, sugar, peppers and coriander or cilantro. Add chicken and marinate for 1 hour.
- Prepare chicken stock with bones, onion, carrots, parsley root and celery. Finely mince or grind the marinated chicken through a meat grinder to a mixing bowl. Add shallots or onion and coriander. To taste for seasonings, make a little patty and sauté it in a skillet; then taste and add whatever you fill is needed.
- To make the galantine: Using a needle with a white thread, sew up the sides of the breast skin pieces, living an opening. Loosely fill with the meat mixture and sew up the opening. Shape to rolls with your hands.
- If you'll have leftover filling or the skin pieces are too small, wrap it in cheese cloth as a roll and tie both ends.
- Carefully lower all the rolls into the stock and simmer for about 1 and a half hour. After about half an hour of simmering, prick a few halls in the rolls, which are in the chicken skin, with a fork. This step will allow the stock to penetrate and moisten the filling.
- When the rolls are cooked, transfer them to a colander and cool to room temperature; then refrigerate for 24 hours. (I like to brown the rolls in the oven or in a skillet, on all sides, for color and crispy skin and then cool and refrigerate them). Slice into 1/2-inch slices.
- To cook as a Pate: Preheat the oven to 375 degrees F. Prepare a deep roasting pan for "au Bain Mare"
- You may like to add to the chicken mixture about 4 ounces of chicken liver or veal or steeped dried mushrooms and mince or grinned altogether.
- Pour the 2 tablespoons oil into ceramic terrine dish with a lid or moisten with a little water and lay a large piece of plastic wrap; then top

with the Pate mixture, smooth the top and tap on the counter to release air bubbles.
- Cover with the lid, place into the roasting pan, transfer to the middle rack of the oven and carefully fill the pan with hot water about half way of the terrine.
- Bake for about 1 and ½ hour, adding water if needed. Cool to room temperature and then refrigerate overnight. Slice and serve on a beautiful platter or tray.

21. Chicken Liver Pate With Bourbon, Honey, And Sage

Serving: Makes 2 cups or so | Prep: | Cook: | Ready in:

Ingredients

- 4 tablespoons butter
- 3 large shallots, sliced
- 1 pound chicken livers, trimmed
- 1 1/2 teaspoons kosher salt
- 1/4 teaspoon allspice
- 1/2 teaspoon freshly ground black pepper
- 1/4 cup loosely packed fresh sage leaves
- 1/4 bourbon
- 1 teaspoon honey, or to taste
- 2 tablespoons melted butter

Direction

- In a large sauté pan, heat the butter over medium-high heat until melted. Add the shallots and cook until translucent. Add the livers, sprinkle with salt, allspice, and pepper. Add sage leaves. Cook for about 2-3 minutes, turning livers occasionally. Add bourbon and increase heat to high. Cook until liquid in pan is almost, but not quite, evaporated.
- Remove liver mixture from heat and place in food processor bowl. Add honey. Pulse until smooth. Pack paté into 2 cup mold or individual ramekins. Pour melted butter over top. Cover and refrigerate for up to three days. Flavor improves as it sits.

- Serve with crusty bread.

22. Chicken Liver Paté

Serving: Serves 6-8 | Prep: | Cook: | Ready in:

Ingredients

- 1 pint chicken livers
- 1 tablespoon butter
- 1 cup milk (enough to cover livers)
- 1 medium onion, chopped
- 4 eggs
- 4 tablespoons chicken fat
- 1/8 cup cognac (optional)
- parsley

Direction

- Rinse livers, trim the sinewy bits, and then soak in milk in the fridge for a couple hours. Rinse, pat dry. Season with salt and pepper, then brown in butter until barely pink inside.
- Add cognac to pan and simmer until evaporated. Cool.
- Bring eggs to a boil, turn off heat, cover and let sit 6 minutes. Rinse under cold water, peel, set aside.
- Finely chop onions and slooowwwwwllllly brown onions in chicken fat or butter (I have also used duck fat) with a pinch of salt until very, very brown. Almost black, they are so slowly and perfectly browned.
- My dad would now just put the livers and eggs through a meat grinder and stir in the fat and onions, season and be done. For me, the grainy texture was never appealing, so I put the livers, onions, 2 eggs, s&p into the Cuisinart and blended until smooth adding about 4 tablespoons of fat a pinch at a time until it was incorporated and velvety. I also stirred in some chopped parsley.
- Finally, separate the whites and yolks of the remaining eggs and push them through a sieve decorating the top of the paté like an egg.

- I served this with slices of grilled baguette brushed with oil but my dad served them with "tiny rye breads" or saltines which are equally good.

23. Chicken Liver Spread (née Pâté)

Serving: Makes 1 cup | Prep: | Cook: | Ready in:

Ingredients

- 7 ounces chicken livers
- 3 tablespoons unsalted butter
- 1 shallot, finely chopped
- 1 sprig rosemary
- 1 tablespoon capers, rinsed and dried
- 2 tablespoons dry vermouth
- 1 teaspoon red wine vinegar
- Coarse salt

Direction

- In a frying pan, melt the butter over medium-low heat. Add the shallot and the rosemary sprig and cook for about five minutes, until the shallot has softened. (It should smell heavenly.)
- Meanwhile, dry the livers and season with salt and pepper. After the shallot has softened, add the livers to the pan and cook for about three minutes per side, or until they're just pink in the middle. Take the pan off the heat and transfer the livers and shallots to a food processor. (Discard the rosemary.) Add the capers to the liver and shallot mixture.
- Return the pan to the heat and add the vermouth. Bring the vermouth to a boil and deglaze the pan, scraping the brown bits off the bottom. When the vermouth has reduced by half, add 1/2 teaspoon coarse salt and the vinegar. Stir and then add to the food processor along with the livers.
- Pulse the food processor until you have a coarse paste. Taste for seasoning and serve.

24. Chicken Livers With Jalapenos

Serving: Makes 1 lb. of chicken livers | Prep: | Cook: | Ready in:

Ingredients

- 2 tablespoons olive oil
- 1 pound chicken livers
- 2 jalapenos, finely julienned
- 1 clove garlic, minced
- salt and pepper
- 2 green onions, sliced
- 1/4 cup cilantro, chopped
- 1/2 lime

Direction

- Heat the oil in a 9-inch skillet over medium to medium high heat.
- Rinse and drain the chicken livers, patting dry as needed.
- Add the chicken livers, jalapenos and garlic to the hot pan. Cook, stirring gently but mainly just turning the livers over. Stirring too hard will result in in more of a pate texture. Season with salt and pepper.
- When the chicken livers are cooked through, add the green onions and cilantro. Stir gently. Squeeze the juice from the half lime over the chicken livers.

25. Chicken Livers With Leeks And Kale

Serving: Serves 4 | Prep: | Cook: | Ready in:

Ingredients

- 4 slices uncured bacon
- 1 pound chicken livers
- 1 cup small chopped leeks
- 2 cups kale cut into ribbons

- salt and pepper to taste
- 1/2 cup chicken broth
- 1 tablespoon flour or arrowroot flour
- 1 clove minced garlic

Direction

- Begin by cooking your bacon in an uncoated pan over medium heat until it's crispy. Remove from the pan and set aside on a paper towel to blot up excess grease.
- Prep your vegetables while the bacon is cooking. Leeks tend to hold onto dirt and grit, so it's important to wash them well. Since the leeks are being chopped, the easiest way to wash them is to start by cutting off the leafy top. Leave the end with the roots intact. Then cut them lengthwise, starting about an inch above the root end. After you've made your first cut, give the leek a quarter turn and cut it in half again, so that it's now cut into 4ths but still held together at the end with the roots, Now you can fan them out under running water and wash off the dirt. Once they're clean, just chop them up and discard the root end.
- For the kale, cut the stem out and then cut each leaf into ribbons lengthwise.
- After removing the bacon from the pan, reserve about 2 Tbsps. of bacon grease and then add the leeks and kale to the pan. Cook over medium heat until they begin to soften for about 3 minutes.
- Turn the heat up to high and brown the liver for 2 minutes on each side for a total of 4 minutes.
- While the liver is cooking, prep what will be your light gravy. In a small bowl whisk together chicken broth, flour or arrowroot flour, and garlic.
- Add the chicken broth mixture to the pan once the liver has browned. You'll notice that it will immediately start sizzling. While it is sizzling, run a wooden spoon along the bottom of the pan. This will pull up drippings and add flavor to your dish. Continue to cook until the sizzling stops and the dish is simmering. At this point, remove the pan from the heat and serve immediately.

26. Chicken Or Rabbit In Creamy Dill & Garlic Sauce

Serving: Serves 6 | Prep: | Cook: |Ready in:

Ingredients

- 1 young rabbit, cut into serving portions, or 2-3 lbs of boneless chicken or turkey thigh
- 2 tablespoons all-purpose unbleached flour
- salt and freshly ground black pepper
- 3 tablespoons butter for browning the meat
- 1 cup chicken stock or white wine, divided in half
- 1 cup sour cream
- 4 cloves garlic, minced
- 1 very large bunch of fresh dill weed, finely chopped

Direction

- Cut up the meat, season liberally with salt and pepper, set aside for about 10 minutes.
- Sprinkle flour over the meat pieces and turn to coat all over.
- Melt butter in a large skillet or Dutch oven over medium/high heat, until lightly brown and bubbly.
- Drop the meat pieces into the butter and brown on all sides until golden and no raw sides are showing anywhere. Add 1/2 cup of wine or stock and scrape the bottom of the skillet with a spatula to deglaze. Stir well.
- When the wine is almost out, add the remaining wine or stock, sour cream, garlic, and all but a handful of chopped dill. Stir very well until smooth and creamy.
- Reduce heat to simmer. Taste for salt and adjust if necessary.
- Cover snugly and simmer for about 15-20 minutes, until meat is tender. Add remaining dill, stir once and serve.

27. Chili Aioli Buffalo Sliders

Serving: Makes 16 | Prep: | Cook: | Ready in:

Ingredients

- 2 pounds ground bison
- 2 large poblano peppers
- 1 alapeno pepper
- 3 hatch chili or anaheim peppers
- 3 loves garlic, minced
- 1 1/2 cups mayonnaise
- 1 lemon
- 1/4-1/2 teaspoons kosher salt (use 1/4, then if more is needed add to your taste.)
- 1/4 pound bacon
- slider rolls
- Colby or jack cheese slices
- sliced tomato
- romaine, iceberg or boston lettuce
- red onion slices
- thinly sliced jalapeño peppers
- sliced avocado

Direction

- Preheat the grill to 450 degrees and place the peppers directly on the grates. (See note below if you don't have a grill) Cook until the peppers are blackened and blistered all over, then transfer to a bowl and cover with plastic wrap until cool enough to handle. Peel the peppers and remove the stem and seeds. Place the peppers in the bowl of a mini-prep food processor. Add the garlic and pulse until peppers are finely minced.
- Mix the peppers and mayonnaise in a medium bowl, stirring until well combined. Using a micro plane grater, zest the lemon. Add the zest to the pepper mixture. Cut the lemon in half and squeeze the juice from half the lemon into the pepper mixture. Season with kosher salt to taste. Refrigerate until ready to use.
- Cut the bacon into 2"-3" pieces and place in a cold cast iron skillet. Heat the skillet over medium to medium high heat, cooking the bacon and flipping it occasionally until crisp and golden. Transfer the bacon to a platter lined with paper towels or newspaper and let the bacon drain. Set the pan aside, but don't drain the bacon fat.
- Divide the buffalo meat into 16 equal portions and gently form them into balls (don't overwork the meat).
- Working in batches, heat the cast iron skillet over medium high heat and when the bacon fat is good and hot, carefully place a few meat balls into the pan. Use a spatula or burger press to flatten the burger to about 1/2" thick. Do this for each of the burgers in the pan. Cook 1-2 minutes and carefully flip the burgers to cook the other side. 1-2 minutes per side for medium rare.
- Transfer the burgers to a platter and continue to cook the other burgers.
- To assemble the sliders, add a heaping tablespoon of the chili aioli to the bottom bun, add a slice of tomato, the burger, cheese, jalapeños, 1-2 slices of cooked bacon and lettuce and other accompaniments.
- Note: If you have a gas stovetop, you can place the peppers directly over the flame to char them. If you don't have a grill or gas stove, preheat the oven to 400 degrees, place peppers on a sheet pan and cook until, blackened on the outside, about 20-30 minutes, then proceed with the recipe.

28. Cocoa Coriander Chili From Jenn De La Vega

Serving: Serves 6 | Prep: 12hours0mins | Cook: 2hours30mins | Ready in:

Ingredients

- 1 pound (450 g) dry red beans
- 1 dried ancho chile

- 1 pound (0.5 kg) ground beef
- 2 tablespoons (30 ml) heavy cream
- Olive oil
- 1 large yellow onion, chopped
- 1 clove garlic, grated
- 1/8 cup (15 g) cocoa powder
- 1/2 tablespoon (5 g) coriander seeds, toasted and crushed
- 1 tablespoon (10 g) masa harina (see Note)
- Salt
- 1 bay leaf
- 1 smoked ham hock (see Note)
- 4 plum tomatoes, chopped (feel free to use canned whole peeled, chopped)
- 2 small Jamaica or Scotch Bonnet peppers, chopped (see Note)
- 1/2 teaspoon ground cumin
- 1 quart (950 ml) beef broth
- 1/4 cup (60 ml) plain yogurt
- 1 bar dark chocolate

Direction

- Wash the red beans, cover with cold water and soak overnight.
- Boil 1 cup water and soak the ancho chile for 20 minutes in it until it is soft. Remove and mince the pepper, keeping the seeds in if you want their rustic texture and flavor and discarding the stem. Fold the minced pepper into the ground beef and heavy cream. Cover and refrigerate for 4 hours or overnight.
- The next day, drain the beans and set aside.
- Sauté the yellow onion for 3 minutes on medium heat with a swirl of olive oil, until it is translucent. Add the ground beef and break it up as it cooks. Once the beef is browned, add the garlic, cocoa, coriander, masa harina, salt, and bay leaf. Stir to combine.
- Turn up the heat to high. Add the drained beans, ham hock, tomatoes, Jamaica peppers, cumin, and beef broth. Bring the chili to a boil and lower to a simmer. Cover and cook for 1 1/2 to 2 hours, until the beans are tender (not chalky). Add salt to taste. If you'd like the chili brothier, add more water or beef broth. If you'd like the chili to be thicker, add more masa harina or see the tip below in step 7. At this point, the ham hock has done its job here—feel free to break it up into the chili or save it for breaking into fried rice, simmering for a broth, or another use.
- Garnish with a dollop of yogurt and grate chocolate over every bowl with a micro plane.
- Note: If you can't find some of the ingredients, you have options! For the masa harina, feel free to leave it out and, at the end, scoop out some of the chili, mash some of the softened beans, and stir it all back in till the chili is as thick as you like. For the Jamaica peppers, feel free to substitute another spicy fresh pepper, like jalapeño (and it *will* be spicy). For the ham hock, a couple chopped slices of bacon are a good alternative.

29. Confit Of Duck Gizzards

Serving: Serves 8 | Prep: | Cook: |Ready in:

Ingredients

- 2.2 pounds fresh duck gizzards
- 2.2 pounds duck fat
- 1 handful coarse salt
- 3 pieces garlic cloves
- 1 piece dried laurel
- 1 piece thyme branch

Direction

- Mix gizzards with the coarse salt and let it marinate for 12 hours in the refrigerator.
- Rinse the gizzards thoroughly and make sure they are dry thereafter.
- Heat the duck fat in a large pot. Then add the gizzards.
- Add garlic cloves, laurel and thyme to a tea pouch, and add this to the pot.
- Simmer for at least one hour.
- Make sure the gizzards are fully cooked before you let them cool.

- The gizzards can be stored in the refrigerator (covered with grease and protected the air) for up to 2 weeks.
- Before eating, heat them up in a pan for 4 to 5 minutes. They go extremely well with a crisp salad in a light vinaigrette. This time I served them with potatoes in a basil pesto as well.

30. Cooking With Tea! Old Fashion Roasted Chicken

Serving: Serves 4-6 people | Prep: | Cook: | Ready in:

Ingredients

- 6 Chicken Breast or one (1) whole chicken
- 1 tablespoon Lapsang Souchong tea..ground down
- 2 tablespoons Garlic powder, crushed or whole cloves(pressed)
- 1 pinch salt to taste (Kosher or sea salt) optional
- 1 pinch white or black pepper
- 2 splashes oil of choice (drizzled) or 1/2 stick of butter (your choice)
- 1 tablespoon onion powder or freshly sliced onions chopped
- set oven to 350 degrees
- 20 mins -1 hour timing: 20 mins for breast only (until done and tender) do not over cook. Whole chicken place in oven for 1 hour depending on size.
  DO NOT OVER COOK MEAT! Check

Direction

- Rinse all chicken thoroughly. Remove excess fat. Skin can be removed if desired. When cooking whole chicken clean inside and outside removing any feathers, excess fat and unwanted guts.
- Pierce chicken with fork or slightly with a knife (point down and stick). This is so seasoning can penetrate into meat.
- Next ground down loose Lapsang Souchong tea. If you do not have a pestle and mortar, use a bowl and spoon to break up the tea as best you can into a coarse powder. You can also break tea up by using your clean fingers. Roll in between thumb and forefinger. Tea will always be coarse using these methods.
- Now it is time to cook. Using whatever cooking dish or pan you prefer begin seasoning the Chicken. It does not matter in which order you choose to season your meat. Now you have removed the excess water off the chicken (leaving some moisture). Sprinkle the chicken with the above ingredients (one at a time or you can place all DRY ingredients into a shaker or bowl and season your meat. Always remember use the ingredients to whatever your taste buds require. And do not heavily season all at once. Gradually increase seasoning to taste as you taste. A good cook always taste their creation as they go alone and before the finale. Viola!
- Using your dry ingredients season your chicken front and back or inside and outside. The seasoning should then be rubbed into the piecing holes.
- Then after all of your seasoning has been added to initial taste, spray, drizzle or rub oil onto chicken so that the dry ingredients will absorb some of the oil. DO NOT OVER OIL. For butter users let butter set until soft or you can melt butter down and let cool. Gently rub your whole chicken with the oil or butter to aid in an even tone color when cooking. The aroma should be slightly drifting upwards from the oily uncooked bird.
- NOW! It is time to cook. Once you have place it in the oven at 350 degrees you will begin to smell the garlic as the bird heats up. About 20 mins for chicken breast or until done but moist. Whole chicken about 1 hour or until done depending on size. REMEMBER to check chicken periodically to insure it is not getting over cooked. Save your drippings from the cooked bird it makes excellent gravy.
- Viola! Now add Rice or Potatoes and a Green Vegetable and dinner is served. Happy eating.

31. Cornmeal Fried Frog Legs

Serving: Makes as many as you can catch | Prep: | Cook: | Ready in:

Ingredients

- buttermilk for marinade (optional)
- frog legs (as many as you want to eat!)
- 1 cup corn meal
- 1/2 teaspoon salt (or to taste)
- 1/4 teaspoon black pepper
- 1/4 teaspoon cayenne
- pinch of ground clove
- pinch of ground ginger

Direction

- Marinate frogs' legs overnight in buttermilk - not necessary, but a tasty and tenderizing addition.
- Combine cornmeal and spices in a large bowl for dredging. Remove frog legs from marinade and dredge through the corn meal mixture. Fry in small batches at 325 degrees for about 6-7 minutes. Serve with homemade ketchup.

32. Cow Brain

Serving: Serves 4 | Prep: | Cook: | Ready in:

Ingredients

- 1 brain
- 3 tablespoons olive oil

Direction

- Cut up brain
- Heat olive oil
- Stir in brain

33. Crepinettes With Kale And Shallots

Serving: Makes 8 | Prep: | Cook: | Ready in:

Ingredients

- 1 small shallot, minced
- 1 tablespoon unsalted butter
- 2 large handfuls lacinato kale, destemmed and sliced thinly
- 2 pounds ground pork shoulder
- 1/4 cup freshly grated parmesan cheese
- 1/4 teaspoon freshly grated nutmeg
- 1/2 teaspoon lemon zest
- 1/4 teaspoon kosher salt
- 1/4 teaspoon black pepper
- 1/4 cup dry white wine
- 1 large piece caul fat, cleaned (about 1/2 pound)
- 2 tablespoons neutral oil, like vegetable, for cooking

Direction

- Preheat oven to 350° F. In a medium saucepan, sweat the minced shallot in the butter over medium-low heat until it's soft and translucent -- about 5 minutes. Add the kale and cook, stirring constantly until it's wilted and soft, about 3 minutes. Place in fridge to cool.
- Once the kale and shallots have cooled completely, place them in cheesecloth and gently squeeze any excess liquid from the kale (this is optional, but recommended).
- Add shallots and kale to a large mixing bowl with the rest of the ingredients (minus the caul fat and vegetable oil). Knead with clean hands for 5 minutes, or until a sample placed on the underside of your palm sticks for a solid 10 seconds.
- Shape mixture into 15 to 20 evenly-sized meatballs.

- Lay caul fat down on a clean surface and cut out 15 to 20 squares, about 4 inches each. Place meatballs in the squares of caul fat and wrap them gently, making sure the edges are sealed. Gently press down and flatten them into disks.
- Heat the vegetable oil in a large oven-safe sauté pan over medium-high heat. Add the crepinettes and sear them on one side until browned -- about 2 minutes. Turn over and sear the other side for 2 minutes.
- Place pan in the preheated oven for 15 minutes. Serve with oysters and wine.

34. Crostini Toscana

Serving: Serves 6 - 10 | Prep: | Cook: |Ready in:

Ingredients

- 3 tablespoons extra-virgin olive oil
- 1 medium red onion, finely diced
- 8 ounces chicken livers
- 1 tablespoon salt-packed capers, rinsed and drained
- 4 salted anchovy fillets, well-rinsed and patted dry and roughly chopped
- 2 tablespoons tomato paste
- 1/2 cup dry red wine
- salt and pepper to taste
- 12 slices of rustic country bread, toasted

Direction

- In a large sauté pan, over medium heat, heat the olive oil. Add diced onion. Cook until soft, but not brown.
- Add chicken livers, capers and anchovies. Cook until lightly browned.
- Add the wine, tomato paste and simmer until reduced to almost dry.
- Pulse the mixture into a food processor until blended but still lumpy -- it should NOT be smooth like a puree.
- Season to taste with salt and pepper and remove to a small mixing bowl.
- Spread each piece of toasted bread with 1 heaping tablespoon of the liver mixture.

35. Day After Casserole For A Hearty Breakfast

Serving: Serves about 6 to 8 | Prep: | Cook: |Ready in:

Ingredients

- • 2 cups leftover meat (turky,beef, pork, chicken, lamb or sausages) chopped in bite-size pieces
- • 2 tablespoons olive oil
- • 1 medium onion diced
- • 1 large or two small leeks (white part) sliced
- • 2 large garlic cloves minced
- • 2-3 medium zucchini unpeeled or 1 large eggplant cut in half and sliced in ¼ -inch pieces
- • 2 cups can tomatoes, drained
- • 1 cup good quality red wine
- • 1 cup fresh or frozen peas
- • ¼ teaspoon ground cinnamon
- • ¼ teaspoon nutmeg freshly ground
- • 2 teaspoons salt
- • ½ teaspoon red pepper flakes
- • 1/2 a pound pasta of your choice fresh cooked or leftover (al dente), I like Pappardelle
- • ½ cup grated Parmesan, Romano or Sharp White Cheddar cheese
- • 2-3 tablespoons fresh herbs of your choice(chopped)

Direction

- Brown the meat in oil; add onion, leeks, and salt; sauté until tender. Stir in zucchini, tomatoes, garlic, and wine, cinnamon, nutmeg, and red pepper flakes; sauté for about 10 minutes or until the mixture is reduced in half. Set aside to cool to room temperature.
- Meanwhile cook pasta; before draining reserve ½ cup of the cooking liquid. If using leftover pasta, worm it in a double boiler. Gently mix

everything together; fold in the fresh peas, chopped herbs, and cheese. If you fill that the mixture needs more moisture, add the reserved cooking liquid.
- Taste for seasoning; grease a four-quart casserole baking dish; pour the mixture, smooth-out the top. In a small bowl combine ½ cup Panko breadcrumbs, 1 tablespoon Extra Virgin olive oil and some more grated cheese. Sprinkle over the top and bake for 30 minutes in 400 degrees preheated oven.

36. Dirty Rotten Roman Risotto

Serving: Serves 4 | Prep: | Cook: | Ready in:

Ingredients

- 1/4 pound chicken gizzards
- 1/4 pound chicken hearts
- 1/4 pound chicken livers (to be cooked separately)
- 1/4 cup guanciale or pancetta, chopped
- 1 rib celery plus leaves, chopped (set the leaves aside)
- 1/2 cup tomato puree (if I were in Roma I would use passata, which is looser than American puree but you can thin it with a little wine if you like)
- 1 teaspoon fresh thyme
- 1/2 cup chopped red onion or shallot
- 1 clove garlic, minced
- 1/4 cup white wine
- 1 1/2 cups Arborio or carnaroli rice
- 5 cups good chicken stock
- extra virgin olive oil
- about 2 ounces butte
- salt and pepper

Direction

- Chop the giblets but hold the livers separately. Ditto for the guanciale/pancetta
- In a sauté pan heat up olive oil to a shimmer not a smoke. Begin by adding the chopped guanciale and let the fat melt a bit. Add the giblets but not the livers (we're holding those back). Brown these on a medium low flame while you begin the rice. Season with salt and pepper and toss in the fresh thyme. Add the chopped celery. Wait a minute or two and add the tomato puree and keep that bubbling.
- Bring the stock to a steady simmer (not a boil) on a burner close to the one on which you will be cooking your risotto.
- Heat up the oil in a large pan, one that will contain the risotto. Add the chopped onions and allow those to color but not brown. Stir in the rice and stir until it begins to become translucent. Add the wine and reduce down. At this point begin ladling in the stock, stirring with each ladleful.
- As the rice absorbs the liquids continue to add more stock, ladle by ladle. After about 8 or 10 minutes add the giblets and sauce and continue the process.
- Meanwhile in a separate pan melt some butter. This will all make sense in the end. Color the garlic and sauté the chopped livers. Before the rice reaches the perfect al dente point add livers to it and stir. From here on it's just taste and season. You add the chicken liver at the end because it's the most delicate component.
- The risotto should still be wet and as they say in Venice, "al onda" meaning "a wave", not a clump of sticky rice. That's another show. Garnish with the chopped celery leaves you have reserved.
- Note to cooks: in Rome you may see big hunks of celery in plates as opposed to dainty little slices. Make up your own mind. You don't have to be a food stylist.

37. Double Cut Wild Caught Venison Chops With Plum And Guajillo Chile BBQ Sauce

Serving: Serves 4 | Prep: | Cook: | Ready in:

Ingredients

- 4 double-cut Frenched venison chops
- 1 1/2 tablespoons extra virgin olive oil
- 3/4 cup yellow onion, minced
- 2 teaspoons garlic, minced
- 1/2 pound small red plums, grand rosa would be nice, pits removed
- 6 guajillo chiles, (these are dried) stems removed and seed, then cut into thin strips
- 1/2 cup water
- 1 tablespoon brown sugar
- 3 tablespoons honey, a light variety prefered
- 1/4 cup cider vinegar
- 2 tablespoons tomato sauce
- Kosher salt and fresh ground pepper

Direction

- Season the chops with salt and place them on a rack and put them in the fridge.
- Place a medium sized sauce pan over medium heat add the chiles and toast them lightly. Remove them from the pan and then add the olive oil and onions to the pan. Sweat the onions until they begin to soften. Add the garlic and plums and then season with a little salt and fresh ground pepper. Once the plums begin to give up their juices add the chiles, water, brown sugar, honey, cider vinegar and tomato sauce.
- Bring to a boil and reduce the heat to a simmer and simmer until the chiles are softened. Remove the sauce from the heat and let it cool.
- Place the sauce into the bowl of a food processor and puree until smooth. Place a strainer over a bowl and pass the sauce through the strainer to remove any chile skins, plum skins and seeds. Rinse the sauce pan and place the sauce back into the pan.
- Heat your grill for direct heat grilling. Season the chops with fresh ground pepper. Grill the chops to rare and remove them to let them rest for 10 minutes. While they are resting warm the BBQ sauce and taste it. Adjust the seasoning if necessary. Put the chops back on the grill and finish the chops by cooking them no further than medium or the venison will be dry. Plate and serve immediately.

38. Duck Bacon Topped Dates Stuffed W/Whiskey Infused Chipotle Sweet Potatoes

Serving: Makes 40 appetizers | Prep: | Cook: | Ready in:

Ingredients

- 2 large sweet potatoes
- 10 slices duck bacon
- 1/2 cup (1 stick) unsalted butter
- 1 tablespoon light brown sugar
- 1/4 teaspoon ground nutmeg
- 1/4 teaspoon ground cinnamon
- 1/8 teaspoon ground ginger
- 1/8 teaspoon kosher salt
- 1 tablespoon bourbon whiskey
- 2 tablespoons chipotle salsa
- 40 medjool dates, pitted

Direction

- Preheat oven to 425 degrees.
- Poke sweet potatoes a few times with the tines of a fork. Then wrap in aluminum foil and bake 1 hour, or until soft and tender.
- While potatoes bake, place duck bacon in a large skillet set over medium heat and cook until done, but not crunchy. When cool enough to touch, cut each slice into 4 evenly sized pieces.
- Melt butter in a small saucepan set over medium heat.
- Add brown sugar, nutmeg, cinnamon, ginger & salt. Whisk until sugar is completely dissolved.
- Remove saucepan from heat and add the bourbon whiskey. With a stick lighter or match, light the liquid and allow the alcohol to burn off.
- Remove from heat and set aside.

- Remove potatoes from the oven and peel off the outer skin.
- Place potatoes and chipotle salsa in a bowl and mash with a potato masher until smooth.
- Add the contents of the saucepan and stir to thoroughly combine.
- Place filled and topped dates on a parchment lined sheet pan, reduce oven temperature to 350 degrees, and bake dates 15 minutes.
- Allow to cool slightly (4-5 minutes) before serving.
- Enjoy.

39. Duck Bolognese

Serving: Serves 4 | Prep: | Cook: | Ready in:

Ingredients

- 300 grams duck meat (aiguilettes de canard or 1 duck thigh)
- 300 grams ground beef
- 6-8 medium tomatoes
- 2-3 finely chopped shallots
- 2 finely chopped garlic cloves
- 1 bay leaf
- 1 handful fresh thyme, rosemary and/or oregano
- 100 milliliters approx. of red wine (1 small glass)
- 100 grams chopped chicken liver
- a few tbsp olive oil
- 1 teaspoon butter + a pinch of flour to drench the liver
- fine salt/fleur de sel + freshly ground pepper to taste

Direction

- Remove strunk from the tomatoes and incise skin crosswise. Place them in a large bowl and pour very hot water on them. Wait until the skin loosens (about 15 minutes), then peel tomatoes, drain well and set aside.
- Peel and chop shallots and garlic.
- Chop the duck meat with a large, very sharp knife. You should obtain very small bits, like a coarse "crumble".
- In a cast iron cocotte, heat a few tbsp. of olive oil. Fry shallots until translucent, 1-2 minutes, add the two meats and continue frying at high heat until well browned and crispy, about 10 minutes. Add garlic and continue frying for 1 minute, stirring frequently.
- Add red wine and reduce until all liquid is gone, vigorously scraping the bottom of your cocotte. Add herbs and tomatoes, crushing them with a fork or spoon. Reduce heat to low, close lid and allow to simmer for 30-40 minutes.
- After 30 minutes, chop chicken liver as finely as possible.
- Heat butter in a small pan over medium heat. Add liver, drench with about ½ tbsp. flour and brown for 3-4 minutes.
- Add to the cocotte, stir and allow to simmer for at least a further 10 minutes.
- Remove herbs and bay leaf and serve with pasta and grated cheese

40. Duck Confit, Pear, And Fennel Bites

Serving: Makes 24 bites | Prep: | Cook: | Ready in:

Ingredients

- 1 sheet puff pastry - defrosted
- 1 duck leg confit - skin removed, meat chopped
- 1 small bulb fennel, chopped
- 1 large firm pear, peeled and chopped
- 1 teaspoon thyme leaves, minced
- 1 clove garlic, minced
- 1 tablespoon olive oil
- 5 ounces brie cheese, rinds included, chopped into 1/2 inch pieces
- 1 tablespoon sherry vinegar

Direction

- Mix on a baking sheet the fennel, pear, thyme, garlic, and olive oil, and season with salt and pepper. Roast for 30 minutes in a 400 degree, preheated oven. Stir 2-3 times. Remove.
- Add chopped duck confit and sherry vinegar to hot cookie sheet. Stir to combine. Taste and season again with salt and pepper if necessary.
- Roll out your thawed puff pastry on a floured work surface to a 12 inch square. Cut the puff pastry sheet into 24 equal pieces. Press each piece into a mini-muffin tin (you'll need more than 1 muffin tin), making a small cup.
- Place 1 square brie cheese in each mini-muffin cup. Add 1.5 teaspoons of the duck, sherry, pear, fennel mixture. Bake in a pre-heated 375 degree oven for 25 minutes. Let cool 5 minutes before serving. Garnish with fresh thyme leaves if desired.

41. Elk Pastrami

Serving: Serves 8-10 as a sandwich | Prep: | Cook: | Ready in:

Ingredients

- For the brine:
- 1 gallon water
- 1/5 cup Kosher salt
- 1 cup brown sugar
- 8 teaspoons pink salt
- 1 teaspoon black pepper
- 1 teaspoon fennel seeds
- 1 teaspoon coriander
- 1 teaspoon clove
- 1 teaspoon cumin
- 6 cloves garlic
- 1/2 cup honey
- 2 sprigs rosemary
- For the pastrami:
- A couple pounds elk meat, shoulder, neck or other cut, preferably bone-in
- 1 tablespoon black pepper
- 1 tablespoon coriander
- 1 tablespoon fennel seed

Direction

- For the brine, bring all those ingredients to a boil and then chill completely. After it is cold, strain out the spices and immerse the elk in the liquid. Continue to brine in the fridge or a cool environment.
- After 3 days, remove the shoulder. Crush the black pepper, coriander and fennel seed and rub the spices into the elk, covering it completely.
- Smoke the shoulder (I used mesquite, but there are any number of possibilities) at 150-180 degrees until the internal temperature of the elk reaches 145. I give you the variation because I am not BBQ master enough to keep the temperature solid. This can take as little as an hour on the side of your grill, or 8 hours using colder smoke. The longer you do it, the more tender it will be - and the smokier.
- Next, set your oven to 280. Cover the bottom of a deep pan with an inch of water, place a bowl or a rack in the bottom of the pan so your elk can sit above the liquid. Set the elk on its rack or pedestal, cover the pan tightly with tin foil and put in the oven for 3 hours, or until the elk is falling off the bone.
- You can serve the pastrami right away, or let cool and then re-steam to serve the next day.

42. Everything Middle Eastern Seasoned Fried Alligator

Serving: Serves 4 | Prep: | Cook: | Ready in:

Ingredients

- 1 pound boneless alligator meat (or chicken is fine)
- 5 cloves of garlic
- 2 teaspoons coriander seeds
- 2 teaspoons baharat

- 1/2 cup whole milk
- 1 cup flour
- 2 cups frying oil (any neutral seed oil)
- Salt to taste
- 2 tablespoons vinegar (I used champagne vinegar)

Direction

- Crush cumin and coriander seeds with mortar and pestle, then mix with the baharat (if you don't have baharat, double the cumin + coriander and add a bit of cinnamon) and salt.
- Cut the meat into bite-size/1.5 inches long pieces and marinade with the spices, chopped up garlic, vinegar, and milk for as long as you like. 15 minutes was enough for me, however.
- Start dredging the pieces in flour (no need to dry off the milk). Fill a small pot or a frying pan with the oil, heat up till 300-400 F and fry. The meat should be cooked in 5 minutes, assuming your pieces are bite-sized.

43. Fab Chicken Liver Pâté

Serving: Serves 6 | Prep: | Cook: | Ready in:

Ingredients

- 8 ounces salted butter
- 1 1/2 onions (4-5 oz.), finely chopped
- 3 garlic cloves, crushed
- 1 pound chicken livers, cleaned and rinsed
- 2 tablespoons brandy
- Salt and freshly ground black pepper
- 1/2 tablespoon pickled green peppercorns, coarsely chopped

Direction

- Gently fry the onions in approx. half the butter until soft and translucent.
- Add the garlic, and cook for one minute more, or until fragrant. Remove onion and garlic from pan with a slotted spoon. Reserve.
- Turn the temperature up, and brown the livers in the remaining butter on all sides. Add brandy, and let reduce a bit.
- Place onions, livers and remaining cold butter in a food processor, and process until smooth. Add salt and pepper to taste. Stir in chopped green peppercorns. Chill in ramekins.

44. Farmer McGregor's Revenge

Serving: Serves 4 | Prep: | Cook: | Ready in:

Ingredients

- 1 Peter Rabbit - cut in 8
- 2 cups carrot juice
- 2 large cloves garlic - thinly sliced
- 1 tablespoon salt (plus more)
- 2 tablespoons fresh thyme leaves
- several sprigs of fresh thyme
- ground pepper
- 2 cups peeled sliced carrots (1/4 inch - the organic ones really are better)
- 1 big leek - cleaned and sliced - white and light green only
- 1 cup flour
- 1 cup dry white wine
- 1 cup chicken broth
- 1/4 cup dry vermouth
- 4-5 bay leafs
- 1 BIG scoop duck fat, enough to generaously coat your pan. I think I used about 1/3 cup

Direction

- Mix together carrot juice, garlic, 1 tbsp. salt, several grinds of pepper and the 2 tbsp. of thyme leaves. Marinate the Peter parts for at least an hour, 2 or 3 is better.
- Turn the oven to 325. Remove the Bunny Bits from the marinade and Pat the Bunny dry (stop, I am killing me here). Season with additional salt and pepper. Heat the duck fat in a big giant skillet or a Dutch oven. Dredge the rabbit in flour, then brown each piece on

both sides in the duck fat. When they have browned remove them to a plate. You will need to do this in 2 or 3 batches.
- Turn the heat down a little and add the carrots and leeks to the pan. Sauté them for a few minutes until they just start to get tender, then add the wine, vermouth and chicken stock. Nestle the bunny into its carroty broth, then spread the thyme sprigs and bay leaf over top. Loosely cover your pan with foil and into the oven for 30 minutes.
- After 30 minutes remove the foil, and continue to cook until the rabbit is tender, mine took an additional 30 minutes - test it by poking with a fork, the fork should go easily to the bone.
- I served my rabbit over polenta - it would also be good on pasta or rice or risotto with peas (which is how I will eat the leftovers tonight!) Also I drank a Bordeaux with this last night and it was really good.

45. Fig Bindenfleisch Crumble With Crottin De Chavignol

Serving: Serves 4 | Prep: | Cook: | Ready in:

Ingredients

- 12 fresh figs
- 4 crottin de Chavignol
- 100g slices of Bindenfleisch
- 3 ounces diced butter
- 4 ounces wholewheat flour
- 2 ounces porridge oats
- 2 tablespoons grated parmesan
- 2 tablespoons ground walnuts
- Salt and pepper

Direction

- Preheat oven on 350F
- In a bowl, combined diced butter, parmesan, flour and ground walnuts. Mix with your fingers to make sure all of the ingredients are combined and crumbly. Add more butter or dried ingredients if needed. Season with salt and pepper.
- Cut the figs in four and place in an oven dish. Cover the entire surface. Season with some pepper. Cut the goat cheese in slices and place on top of the figs. Top with the slices of meat, cover the entire surface.
- Pour the crumble on top of the filling.
- Bake for about 30 minutes

46. Foie Gras Butter Pan Roasted Lamb Chops With Pistachio Fennel Dust

Serving: Serves 2 | Prep: | Cook: | Ready in:

Ingredients

- 4 long rib lamb chops
- 2 Inch cut from a foie gras terrine
- 3 Inch cut of yellow french butter
- 1/8 cup unsalted shelled pistachios
- 1/8 cup fennel seeds
- 1 tablespoon kosher salt
- 1 teaspoon crushed black tellicherry peppercorn

Direction

- Make sure the lamb chops are well cleaned, removing any sinew (white covering attached to the chop. Trim some of the fat off the chop handle if it's overly thick but be sure to leave some fat, as this is the delicious, crispy part you will want to indulge in later.
- Blend 2 inch equal parts of the room temperature yellow French butter foie gras terrine and pinch of kosher salt with a fork until the two have an evenly colored consistency. Microwave the mixture for 15 seconds (just enough to liquify the mixture).
- Using a brush (or I prefer hand), massage the mixture into each chop, both chop and handle. Apply pinch of kosher salt to each side of the chop. Let rest uncovered for 15 minutes.

- In a medium heat pan (prefer tin lined copper) add 1 inch of the cut yellow butter to the pan, careful not to burn the butter. Add the chops in opposing orientations so all 4 chops fit in the pan. As one side crisps and browns, you will see a tannish- brown butter form. Let the one side cook untouched for approximately 3 minutes.
- Lower the heat and tilt the pan so that the foie gras butter pools at the bottom and the chops are largely off the heat at the top. Spoon the mixture over the chops repeatedly for approximately 2-3 minutes. Flip the chops over and repeat, allowing the other side to also cook untouched for approximately 2 minutes before spooning the mixture over.
- Sprinkle a finely blended (in a spice grinder) mixture of the pistachio and fennel seeds over the chops. I like to lightly toast the mixture for 1 minute in a dry pan to release the oils from the mixture. Do not burn the mixture. The mixture will adhere to the chops and handle.
- Remove the chops from the pan and plate. No need to let the chops rest for more than a minute. Add a sprinkle of the black tellicherry pepper. You may spoon over the residual butter or serve alongside a crispy bread.

47. Foie Gras Au Gros Sel

Serving: Makes 1 log of foie gras | Prep: | Cook: | Ready in:

Ingredients

- 1 raw "fat" duck or goose liver
- freshly grated black pepper
- 1/2 cup Cognac or Armagnac
- 2.2 pounds large-grain sea salt

Direction

- Place the duck or goose liver on a large plate or cutting board. "Unfold" both parts of the liver. With your fingers and with a knife, carefully remove any white veins or connective tissue, without making too many holes liver. Sprinkle the inside of both parts with freshly ground black pepper before folding to two halves back on top of each other.
- Pour the Cognac or Armagnac into a shallow bowl. Wet a large piece of cheesecloth completely, then wring it out and lay it on a flat surface. Place the liver on top of the cheesecloth, and then roll the cheesecloth tightly around the liver. You want it to resemble a log, so shape it with your hands as you roll. When you are happy with the shape, tuck the ends of the cheesecloth under.
- Inside the terrine, layer about 1 inch of sea salt. Place the cheesecloth package on top of the salt, and then cover it completely with the rest of the salt. (The cheesecloth should be completely covered on all sides, so make sure the terrine is big enough that there is space to encase the liver completely).
- Wrap the top of the terrine in plastic, and place it in the refrigerator for 48 hours. (This is important—less than 48 hours and the foie gras won't be "cooked," longer than 48 hours and you risk over salting it).
- After 48 hours, remove the plastic wrap, and take out the cheesecloth. (The salt can be reserved for another use.) Dust any excess salt from the cheesecloth, and then unwrap. Serve the foie gras with pain de mie. (Or any buttery bread.)

48. Foie Gras, Roasted Figs With Raspberry Vinaigrette

Serving: Serves 4 | Prep: | Cook: | Ready in:

Ingredients

- Salad
- 4 slices of Foie Gras
- 8 Fresh figs, black

- 8 green salad leaves
- 4 red salad leaves
- 2 pinches Fleur de Sel or Black Salt
- 2 pinches light brown sugar
- Raspberry Vinaigrette
- 6 tablespoons Extra Virgin Olive Oil
- 3 tablespoons Balsamic Vinegar
- 1 teaspoon honey
- salt
- pepper
- 12 Raspberries fresh

Direction

- For the Vinaigrette: In a beaker add all the ingredients and process with an immersion blender for 30 seconds or until creamy.
- Add the raspberries and process another 30 seconds so you can still see the seeds.
- Check for seasoning and set aside.
- For the salad: Pre-heat the oven to 400°F.
- Wash and dry the salad leaves and keep in a clean kitchen tea towel in the fridge.
- Cut the stems of the figs and cut them in a rose, slicing them in quarters but leaving the bottom intact. Sprinkle with the brown sugar and roast in a parchment paper lined baking try for 15 minutes.
- Plate your entrée, sprinkle some Fleur de Sel or Black Salt on the foie gras and drizzle with some Raspberry vinaigrette. Serve immediately.

49. Fried Rice With Duck Confit And Celeriac

Serving: Serves 2 | Prep: | Cook: | Ready in:

Ingredients

- 4 Duck Legs Confit
- 2 cups white Rice
- 1 cup celeriac, 1/2" cubed or sliced
- 1 tablespoon butter
- 1 lemon, for zest

Direction

- Preheat the oven to 350. Melt the butter on med heat in a skillet, add rice. Sauté the rice 5 min, then add celeriac. Set skillet in the oven for 5- 10 min, until celeriac is cooked but still firm. While the skillet is in the oven, take the confit out of the fat and shred. (I find it helpful to warm the fat again until it is liquid) Replace skillet to stove and add leeks and duck. Continue to sauté until heated through. Portion to serve, and garnish with lemon zest.

50. Giblet Gravy

Serving: Serves 10-12 | Prep: | Cook: | Ready in:

Ingredients

- Innards (heart, liver, neck, and whatever else is packaged inside the cavity of your bird) from one turkey (these are the giblets)
- 2 eggs, hardboiled
- drippings from turkey roasting pan
- chicken stock
- 2 tablespoons cornstarch
- 1/2 medium onion, diced fine
- salt and pepper to taste

Direction

- Boil the turkey neck, heart, liver and so on, along with the chopped onion in about 2 cups of water with a dash of salt and pepper until they're done. Remove giblets, and reserve broth.
- Give the neck to your dog, who will love you forever for it. Chop the remaining giblets into about 1/4 inch dice, and return to saucepan with broth.
- Peel and chop hardboiled eggs, crumble yolk, and add to broth.
- To about 1/4 cup chicken broth, add the 2 tablespoons of cornstarch and stir until smooth.

- Pour drippings from turkey roasting pan into saucepan. Bring the whole thing to a boil, and lower heat to medium. Stir in cornstarch slurry.
- Add enough more chicken broth to make about however much gravy you think you'll want. (If you're going up higher than 12, you needed another turkey anyway, and therefore will have more giblets. Use them, add an egg, and add another tablespoon of cornstarch.)
- Simmer until thick, and serve.

51. Goat Ragout With Figs & Rosemary Over Pappardelle

Serving: Serves 4-6 | Prep: | Cook: | Ready in:

Ingredients

- 2 pounds bone-in goat stew meat
- 2 large onions, diced
- 3 medium carrots, diced
- 4 cloves garlic, chopped
- 3 tablespoons olive oil
- 1 tablespoon chopped fresh rosemary
- 1 tablespoon chopped fresh thyme
- 1/4 cup roughly chopped Italian parsley
- 1 cup diced dried figs
- 1/4 cup all-purpose flour
- 1/2 cup red wine
- 1 quart beef stock
- 1 quart tomato puree or diced fresh tomatoes
- 1/4 cup cornstarch slurry (1 tbsp cornstarch dissolved in roughly ¼ cup warm water)
- Sea salt
- Freshly ground black pepper
- 1 pound pappardelle pasta, cooked, drained, and tossed with olive oil

Direction

- Preheat the oven to 250°F. Mix the flour with a teaspoon or so of sea salt and a few grinds of black pepper, then dredge the stew meat in it, doing your best to coat all sides with the mixture.
- Heat the oil over medium heat in a Dutch oven (you can also use a wide-bottomed metal pot or sauté pan with high sides, but it must be oven-safe since you'll be finishing this dish in the oven) until it begins to shimmer, then add the meat to the pan, turning it to brown it on all sides— roughly two-three minutes per side. You'll most likely need to do this in two batches to avoid crowding and achieve the proper sear.
- Remove the meat and set it aside in a bowl. Add the onions, carrots, and garlic to the pan and sauté for 3-5 minutes, until the onions start to become translucent and the carrots begin to soften. Deglaze the pan with the red wine, using a wooden spoon to scrape up any odds and ends and ensure that nothing is stuck to the bottom.
- Add the meat back to the pan along with the beef stock and the tomato and bring to a simmer. Add the cornstarch slurry to thicken the sauce and stir thoroughly with a fork to distribute it throughout. Simmer for roughly 5 minutes before adding the chopped herbs and figs, then season with more salt and pepper, cover, and place in the oven for three to four hours, checking a few times to stir and make sure there's enough liquid, until the meat is fork tender. Take the meat off the bones and return the shredded meat to the pot before serving over your favorite pappardelle pasta.

52. Grilled Quail With Sage And Pancetta

Serving: Serves 6 as an hors d'oeuvre | Prep: 0hours30mins | Cook: 0hours6mins | Ready in:

Ingredients

- 6 quail (I get mine at D'Artagnan.com and semi-boneless is easiest!)
- 6 small garlic cloves, peeled

- 6 small bunches fresh sage
- 6 slices pancetta
- 6 large fresh grape leaves
- toothpicks to close grape leaves

Direction

- Rinse quails, inside and out, and dry well with paper towels.
- Crush the garlic cloves with the side of a chef's knife. Put one garlic clove and one small bunch of sage inside each quail. Wrap each quail with a strip of pancetta. Set the whole thing in the center of a fresh grape (or lettuce) leaf. Fold the leaf around the bird to cover completely. Fasten the leaf closed with a toothpick which has been soaked in water for at least one-half hour.
- Grill over smoldering coals for about 3 minutes on each side.
- Teacher's Tip: If you can't find fresh grape leaves, you can use the ones that come in brine in the Middle-Eastern groceries, or use de-veined romaine lettuce leaves.

53. Grilled Wild Goose With A Fire Roasted Corn And Poblano Salsa

Serving: Serves 4 | Prep: | Cook: |Ready in:

Ingredients

- Salsa
- 2 Corn on the Cobs, with husks
- 3 Large Poblanos
- 3 Jalapeños
- 3 tablespoons Cilantro, chopped
- 1 Clove of Garlic, minced
- 1 Lime, juiced
- 1 teaspoon Honey
- 4 tablespoons Avocado Oil (or other neutral oil)
- Goose Sandwich
- 4 Goose Breasts, dry brined (I used Snow)
- 4 Ciabatta Buns
- 1 Avocado, Sliced
- 1 cup Romaine, shredded
- 1 tablespoon Ancho Chili Powder
- 2 teaspoons Brown Sugar
- 1 teaspoon Black Pepper

Direction

- Salsa: Soak the corn, still inside of the husk, for about 30 minutes in a bowl full of water. After the corn has soaked, over a medium-high heat, place corn husks directly on grill. The corn will take longer to cook than the poblanos, about 20 minutes. When the corn husks are dried out starting to burn, remove them from the grill and once they've cooled, peel back the husks. At this point they should be steamed through, but for an extra char you can season with salt, pepper, and rub a little oil over them and place it back on the grill for a few minutes, turning occasionally. Using a sharp knife, slice the corn kernels off the cob lengthwise and place into a bowl. Poblanos: Place the Poblanos directly on the gill next to the corn. Let the poblanos start to roast and blacken, checking and turning every few minutes. Remove the poblanos to a cutting board once they are blackened all the way around and let it cool. Once they've cooled, you can start to peel off the blackened skin from the flesh and scrape off the seeds with a small knife. After fully removing the outer skin and seeds, chop the poblanos and add it to the bowl with the corn. Also add the chopped jalapeños, cilantro and garlic. In a separate, small bowl, whisk together the juice of one lime, honey and the oil. Once the vinaigrette is emulsified, pour all but a few spoonfuls over the bowl of corn and poblanos. Mix the salsa together and set aside to serve. The reserved lime vinaigrette will be used to spoon over the romaine.
- Goose: Once all your prep work for the salsa is done and set aside, mix the Spice mix and rub it into the goose breasts. If you chose to dry-brine your birds like I do overnight with salt,

you will not need to add extra salt to the spice mix. If you did not dry brine the bird, than you should add one teaspoon of salt. If you have the skin on, or a particularly fatty bird, score the skin to allow fat to seep out. If you have a lean, skinless bird, than I like to rub a tiny bit of grape seed/canola oil over the meat and then season with the spice rub. Grill the goose over high heat on each side for approximately 2-4 minutes each side. Your cook time will depend greatly on the size of the bird, I like all of my waterfowl to be between rare and medium rare. Remove and let it rest under foil for 10 minutes to soak up juices, keeping in mind that it will continue to cook a little under the foil. Thinly slice the goose breast for serving.
- Assemble: To serve, slice the ciabatta into toasts and layer with avocado, romaine, lime vinaigrette, sliced goose, and the roasted poblano - corn salsa.

54. Guinea Fowl With Chestnut Stuffing (Faraona Ripiena Di Castagne)

Serving: Serves 4 | Prep: | Cook: | Ready in:

Ingredients

- For the guinea fowl
- 1 guinea fowl (or 2 poussin)
- Salt and pepper
- 2 plain Italian pork sausages
- 20 boiled and peeled chestnuts (approx)
- 8 fresh sage leaves
- 3.5 ounces paper-thin slices of pancetta
- A sauce (optional)
- The wings from the guinea fowl
- 3 to 4 slices of pancetta
- 10 dried porcini mushroom pieces, soaked in hot water
- 1 scallion
- 1 teaspoon tomato paste
- 1 wine glass full of white wine
- 1 teaspoon cold butter

Direction

- Debone the bird, setting aside the wings for the sauce, if making. Season the inside with some salt and pepper.
- Remove the sausage casings and blend the sausage meat with the chestnuts in a food processor, or if you prefer a more rustic filling, finely chop the chestnuts and add to the sausage meat and blend with a fork until well incorporated. Finely chop the sage leaves and add to the mixture. Stuff the bird with this mixture.
- Assemble the pancetta on some parchment or cling wrap, slightly overlapping the slices, to create an even layer the same length as the bird and wide enough to wrap around the bird. Lay the bird in the middle and wrap the parchment around it, so you have a perfect layer of pancetta covering the entire bird. Remove the parchment/cling wrap carefully.
- Truss the bird with trussing string to keep it together in an even shape. Sear the trussed bird in an ovenproof pan until browned on all sides, then place in a hot oven (about 350ºF) for until a meat thermometer shows the internal temperature is 140-150ºF). For the poussin, this was roughly 20 minutes; for guinea fowl or chicken, it will likely take twice as long. I recommend using a thermometer to check doneness. Remove from the oven and let rest, covered, keeping warm.
- Make a sauce to accompany the roast by sautéing the wings with a few slices of pancetta. Brown them well, the browner and stickier they become, the better. Add the revived porcini mushrooms, drained (reserve the liquid), then lower the heat and add the chopped scallion and sauté until soft. Add tomato paste for color and deglaze the pan with the mushroom liquid and white wine. Season with salt and pepper and reduce the sauce until it has thickened slightly. Strain the sauce and return to the pan with the butter,

whisking to incorporate. Serve with the roast, cut into thick slices.
- This would go well with some polenta and a side of seasonal vegetables.

55. Hare With Onions (Stifado)

Serving: Serves 5 | Prep: | Cook: |Ready in:

Ingredients

- For the oven
- 1.5 kilo Hare cut in 10 pieces
- 1.5 kilo dry onions (small 4-5 cm diameter)
- 1 cup Good red wine
- 1/3 cup Wine vinegar
- 1 cup Water
- 1 teaspoon Sugar or wine syrup
- Peel of half an orange
- Salt
- Marinade
- 1 cup Good red wine
- 3/4 cup Wine vinegar
- 1 Cinammon stick
- 6 Cloves
- 2 Bay leaves
- 10 Whole black peppers

Direction

- Put the hare and marinade ingredients in a plastic bag, and place in the fridge for at least 8 hours, more is even better. Turn several times during that period.
- The next day, drain the hare, but keep one cup of the marinade and the spices, to use in the cooking.
- Heat in a deep frying pan, 3/4 of the oil and add the hare. Seal on both sides. Add salt and place in a baking tray with the frying oil.
- In another frying pan add the rest of the oil and fry the onions. Lower the heat a bit and turn so the onions do not burn. Cook for 15 minutes, or until there is some color round them.
- Place the onions on top of the hare, add the spices, orange peel, the marinade, wine, and the water.
- The onions should be on top. Sprinkle some salt and the sugar.
- Cover the tray well with foil, but make a few openings with a skewer on top, so that some steam can evaporate.

56. Harvest Stew

Serving: Serves 6-8 | Prep: 0hours0mins | Cook: 0hours0mins |Ready in:

Ingredients

- 1 tablespoon olive oil
- 1 large onion (peeled & chopped)
- 1/2 head of garlic (peeled & minced)
- 1-1/2 pounds ground bison
- 2 pounds butternut squash (peeled & cubed)
- 30 ounces canned tomato sauce (I like Muir Glen)
- 2 cups vegetable broth
- 1/2 teaspoon sea salt
- 10 ounces fresh baby spinach

Direction

- Chop onion & garlic & place in large soup pot with olive oil. Cook over medium heat for a few minutes, to soften.
- Add bison & brown both sides, cutting meat into chunks in the process.
- Add tomato sauce, broth & salt. Bring to boil & then reduce to simmer.
- Peel & de-seed squash. Chop into cubes & add to pot. Simmer for 30 minutes
- Add baby spinach last, cooking for just 1-2 minutes, until wilted.
- Serve!

57. Home Sweet Home Buffalo Chili

Serving: Serves around 8 | Prep: | Cook: |Ready in:

Ingredients

- The Roux
- 2 tablespoons olive oil
- 2 tablespoons flour
- 1 tablespoon ground cumin
- 2 teaspoons dried oregano
- 2 teaspoons coarse black pepper
- 1 1/2 teaspoons white pepper
- 2 teaspoons crushed red pepper (cayenne or Thai)
- The Chili
- 2 cups onion, large dice
- 4 large garlic cloves, minced
- 1 cup bell pepper
- 1/2 cup garlic stems
- 1 (or 2) jalapeno pepper
- 2 pounds ground buffalo
- 28- ounces can fire-roasted tomatoes, undrained (Meir Glen my favorite)
- 12 ounces dark beer
- 15 ounces can black beans, drained, rinsed
- 2 squares baking chocolate (or Van Houten cocoa)
- salt, to taste
- tortillas or na'an

Direction

- Heat oil in a large cooking pot with a heavy bottom over medium heat. Add flour and stir until the roux is a light caramel color. Lower heat, add spices and stir for 1 minute.
- Add onion and sauté 7 minutes. Add garlic, garlic stems, and peppers, and cook for 3 minutes.
- Add buffalo meat, raise to medium heat and cook until pink is gone. Add tomatoes and beer, and bring to a boil. Cover, reduce heat, and simmer for 1 hour.
- Stir in beans and chocolate, stirring to melt. Add salt to taste. Cook, covered, for 15 minutes.
- Serve with tortillas. My hearty-appitite son likes to eat it with na'an.
- Leave out the beans, vegetarian still great chili. Goes great with toppings: sour cream, cheddar cheese, diced avocado, sliced green onions, or crunchy stuff like corn chips!
- Go Buffalos!

58. Indian Inspired Goat Rillette

Serving: Makes 2 cups | Prep: | Cook: |Ready in:

Ingredients

- 4 to 5 tablespoons ghee (purified butter)
- 2 pounds goat stew meat
- 1 pound pork belly or scraps with fat, cut in 1 1/2 inch cubes
- 1 teaspoon cumin seeds
- 1 large onion, chopped
- 3 cloves garlic, chopped
- 1 tablespoon finely chopped or lightly crushed ginger
- 2 teaspoons ground cumin
- 2 teaspoons ground coriander
- 1 teaspoon turmeric
- 1 teaspoon ground cayenne pepper
- 2 teaspoons salt
- 1 cup water
- 1/4 cup lard
- 10 cloves
- 1 cinnamon stick, 2 inches long
- 2 black cardamom pods
- 3 Green cardamom pods

Direction

- Make sachet with: 10 cloves1 cinnamon stick, 2 inches long2 Black cardamom pods3 Green cardamom pods

- Melt 1tbl of Ghee on medium heat in a large, heavy stockpot. Add cumin seeds and sauté until they sizzle, about 45 seconds.
- Add onions and sauté until golden brown, about 8 to 10 minutes
- Add garlic and sauté 2 to 3 minutes, or until golden brown
- Stir in ginger. After 1 minute, add ground cumin, coriander, turmeric, cloves, cinnamon, cayenne, and salt. Cook on medium heat, stirring regularly, for 5 to 10 minutes or until ghee (or oil) separates from the spices. Add another tablespoon of ghee or oil if spices are sticking to the bottom of the pot. Let cool down and puree all together in Cuisinart. Put aside.
- Melt remaining ghee on medium heat in the same pot. Add pork and goat meat to pot. Mix in the pureed spices and onion. Bring to a simmer. Add sachet, salt and water. Let cook until meat is falling off the bone (about 3 - 4 hours). Add liquid (water, wine, whatever as needed so that the meat doesn't completely dry out but not too much
- When done let cool enough so that you can handle. Remove sachet and any bones. Put meat into Cuisinart and pulse until the meat is a course texture. Put meat into sterilized jars. Let cool overnight. Keeps about 2 weeks. Longer if you add lard to the chilled jars to seal.

59. Jacinta's Duck Rice Arroz De Pato Da Jacinta

Serving: Serves 6 - 8 | Prep: | Cook: | Ready in:

Ingredients

- 4 1/2 pounds whole duck, cut up in 8 pieces
- 2 1/2 cups medium grain rice
- 5 cups duck broth (from cooking the duck)
- 1/2 Chourizo
- 2 medium yellow onions peeled and left whole
- 1 medium carrot
- 1 medium leek – white part only
- 1 celery stalk, trimmed
- 2 garlic cloves, peeled and left whole
- 2 bay leaves
- 3 cloves
- 6 sprigs fresh parsley
- 3 sprigs fresh thyme
- 1 teaspoon Black whole peppercorns
- 2 tablespoons Extra Virgin Olive Oil
- salt

Direction

- Peel the garlic and the onion and leave whole. Insert the cloves in the onion by pressing them in.
- Wash the leek very well to remove any earth attached.
- Peel the carrot. Trim and wash the celery stalk. Wash the parsley and the fresh thyme leaving the stalks.
- Wash the whole duck and cut in 8 pieces.
- In a big pot over high heat, add the duck, onion with cloves, leek, celery stalk, carrot, garlic, bay leaves, parsley, thyme, peppercorns and cover with water. Season with salt. Bring to a boil, reduce the heat and simmer, covered with lid, for 1 hour. Remove the lid and allow to cook for a further 45 minutes until duck is very tender and almost falling of the bones.
- Remove the duck from the broth and let it cool. Remove the flesh, shred it in big pieces. Discard the skin and all the bones – be very thorough because the duck has some very small bones.
- Sieve the duck broth and reserve – you will need 5 cups. The broth will be very rich and have a lot of fat from the duck which will give the rice its special flavor.
- In a big pan with a tight fitting lid, over medium heat, add the olive oil and fry the rice until it's well coated in olive oil and almost sticking to the pan.

- Add the duck broth, stir and scrape any rice attached to the pan. Check the salt, bring to a boil, reduce the heat and simmer, covered, for 17 minutes. During this time DO NOT uncover or stir the rice.
- Remove from the heat and allow to rest for 5 minutes without uncovering the pan or stirring the rice.
- Fluff up the rice so you don't have any lumps.
- Pre-heat the oven to 375'ºF with rack in the middle position.
- In a deep oven proof serving dish, spread half the fluffed up rice. Spread with the shredded duck on top. Cover with the remaining rice.
- Slice the chorizo and add slices on top of the rice.
- Bake in the oven for 8 to 10 minutes until the top layer of the rice is lightly golden and the chorizo is crispy. Serve immediately.

60. Kashmiri Venison Burger

Serving: Serves 4 | Prep: | Cook: | Ready in:

Ingredients

- For the spice mix
- 3   dried Kashmiri chilies
- 1/2 tablespoon coriander seeds
- 1/2 tablespoon cumin seeds
- 2   cardamom pods
- 1/2   star anise
- For the burgers
- 250 grams ground venison
- 2   scallions, thinly sliced
- 1 1/2 tablespoons spice mix (above)
- 2 tablespoons beaten egg
- Salt
- Pepper

Direction

- Toast all the spices for the spice mix in a small skillet until aromatic. This should take only a couple minutes. Remove the spices to a spice grinder or mortar and grind or pound until fine and uniform.
- Combine all the ingredients for the burger and form into patties. Fry on the stovetop in a little oil, or cook them on the grill. Serve on a toasted bun (or on toasted naan).

61. Lemon And Thyme Grouse Piccata

Serving: Serves 4 | Prep: | Cook: | Ready in:

Ingredients

- 4   Skinless, boneless Grouse breast pounding thin (to approximately 1/4")
- 1/4 cup all purpose white flour
- 1/2 teaspoon salt
- 1/2 teaspoon black pepper
- 4 tablespoons butter, divided
- 2 tablespoons Extra Virgin Olive Oil
- 1/2 cup grouse or chicken broth
- 1/3 cup fresh squeezed lemon juice
- 1/4 cup capers, drained and rinsed
- 1 tablespoon fresh thyme, mince
- 2 tablespoons fresh parsley, chopped

Direction

- Mix the flour, salt and pepper in a shallow bowl. Dredge the grouse lightly through the flour.
- In a large saute pan, heat 2 tablespoons of butter and olive oil over medium high heat. Add the grouse and cook for 3 minutes on each side or until golden brown (do not overcook). Set grouse aside on a plate and cover with foil to keep warm.
- Add broth, lemon juice, capers and thyme to the same pan, deglazing the pan. Stir and scrape up any brown bits.
- Return grouse to the pan, cook another 5 minutes. Transfer grouse to a platter. Whisk in the remaining butter into the sauce. Pour over grouse and garnish with parsley.

62. Life Path Paella

Serving: Serves 4 | Prep: | Cook: |Ready in:

Ingredients

- 1 red bell pepper
- 1/2   sweet yellow onion
- 1 heaping teaspoons New Mexico red chili
- 1 pinch saffron
- 1 1/2 cups parboiled rice, I like Zatarains. And listen, no lip about this - it's very forgiving, cooks quickly and works great!
- 2   semi boneless quail
- 1/2 pound black mussels
- 1/2 pound littleneck clams (quahogs!)
- 2   links (6 oz) spanish chorizo
- 1/2 cup frozen peas
- 1/2 cup dry white wine
- 1 tablespoon tomato paste (the double concentrated tube kind)
- 2 cups chicken broth
- olive oil to coat the pan
- salt and pepper
- a handful of chopped flat leaf parsley
- juice from one lemon

Direction

- First, char the bell pepper. I did this over the flame on our gas stove but you could grill it or broil it. Just a light char, not completely blackened. While it cools dice the onion, slice the chorizo, and mince the garlic. Season the quail generously all over with salt and pepper. Now seed the pepper and slice it into strips. Eat a few, they are irresistible and you have plenty.
- Coat the bottom of your paella pan or large skillet with olive oil. Heat to medium-high and put the chorizo in. Brown the chorizo and then remove it with a slotted spoon. Now put the quail in the pan - you want to crisp up the skin but not cook it through, so keep the heat kind of high. When the quail are crisped take them out and set them aside.
- Now you can turn the heat down a little. Add the chili powder and saffron to the pan. Put the onion in and sauté until it softened, then add the garlic and the rice. Cook, stirring, for a few more minutes until the rice is a little toasty. Now add the wine and tomato paste and stir, then broth and stir, then add the chorizo back in, with the peas and peppers. Cut the quail into quarters and nestle them into the rice. Cover the pan and set you timer for 15 minutes.
- You may as well have a glass of wine now. Also go ahead and scrub the clams and the mussels. May as well chop the parsley too. Cut the lemon in half.
- When the timer goes off, open the lid and arrange the clams hinge side down in the rice. Don't push them down too far though or they will have trouble opening. Lid back on, and wait 3 minutes.
- Now arrange the mussels in there as well. Put the lid back on and CRANK the heat to high - this will open the mussels and give you your crisp (Is it called soccorat? I think that's right) at the same time. You can hear it sizzling if you put your ear by the pan. DO NOT catch your hair on fire. This will take just 3 or 4 minutes.
- Finish the paella with a scattering of chopped parsley and a squeeze of lemon. See? Not so hard!
- ** A tip - we (and by "we" I mean Mr. L as he is trying to get all of the crispy stuff for himself) use a metal fish spatula to get the crisp part up **

63. Liver Dumpling Meatballs In A Heavenly Broth

Serving: Serves 4-6 | Prep: | Cook: |Ready in:

Ingredients

- 1 pound chicken livers from organic free range chickens, ground
- 2 eggs, slightly beaten
- 1 cup stale peasant bread crumbs (a little extra as well, in case needed)
- 1/4 cup dry white wine
- 1 ounce shallots, finely minced
- 1 ounce carrots, finely minced
- 1 ounce celeriac, finely minced
- 2 tablespoons chopped flat leaf parsley
- 2 tablespoons flour
- 1 tablespoon butter
- 3/4 teaspoon kosher salt
- 1/4 teaspoon ground white pepper
- 2 tablespoons flat leaf parsley, (or cilantro) chopped, for garnish
- 1 quart homemade soup broth
- sweet paprika for garnish

Direction

- Add your stale bread crumbs to the beaten eggs.
- Make sure your chicken livers have no skins or tissue before grinding. They must be pure. Add to ground livers to the bowl.
- Melt butter in a skillet and add the minced shallot, celeriac, and carrot. Cook until they are softened for about 1 minute, but do not brown. Next stir in the flour, salt, and pepper to the pan. Add the wine and reduce. Then add this whole mixture plus 2 tbsp. parsley to the mix in the bowl.
- Cover and chill the combined mixture until cold (about 4 hours).
- After the mixture is cold, bring your homemade broth to a simmer. Scoop and drop about 20 small balls (@3/4") from the cold mix into the simmering broth.
- The mixture should hold together; if not add a little more bread crumbs. Poach for about 15 minutes, or until they dumplings rise to the top.
- Serve with the broth and garnish with 2 tbsp. fresh chopped parsley (or cilantro) and sweet paprika.

64. Loco Marinade

Serving: Makes more than enough | Prep: | Cook: | Ready in:

Ingredients

- 1 cup pineapple juice
- juice of two limes
- 2 tablespoons white vinegar
- 6 cloves of garlic, sliced or smashed
- 1/4 teaspoon cayenne
- 1 teaspoon dried oregano
- 1 tablespoon turmeric
- 1/4 teaspoon white or black pepper
- 1 teaspoon salt
- 1 bay leaf

Direction

- Combine, garlic, lime juice, oregano, salt and pepper in a blender and puree. You can also use a stick blender for this.
- Add all additional ingredients and mix well.
- Add meat of choice and go! You can freeze any remaining marinade for later OR using for basting on the grill! This makes a huge amount of marinade, enough for an entire whole chicken and then some!

65. MOM'S TURKEY GIBLET GRAVY

Serving: Serves a crowd of thanksgiving guestss | Prep: | Cook: | Ready in:

Ingredients

- turkey parts, (neck, gizzard, pope's nose)
- 1 large onion, chopped
- 1 stalk of celery, chopped
- 1 large carrot, chopped
- large pot of water

- turkey juices in roasting pan
- 3 tbs butter
- 1/2 cup flour
- salt and black pepper to taste
- turkey roasting pan that is NOT non-stick

Direction

- In a large stock pot, put the turkey parts, onion, carrot, celery and fill with water.
- Slowly simmer the stock until the contents are very cooked and the liquid is slightly reduced. Cool and refrigerate until ready for use.
- On the day the turkey is in the oven cooking, heat the turkey stock on low heat and use it to baste the turkey while it is cooking.
- After the turkey has been removed from the oven and is resting, make the gravy.
- Deglaze the roasting pan with some turkey stock and using a spatula, scrape up the caramelized bits on the pan bottom. Chop the giblets very finely and add to the pan and stir.
- Add a large dollop of butter (about 3 tbsp.) to the pan and melt. Then add some flour (about 1/2 cup) and with a fork or whisk blend really well very quickly to prevent lumps from forming. It is important to not have any lumps at this stage.
- Then, add some more stock to the pan and stir, stir and keep stirring! If it is too thick, add more stock and stir some more.
- The gravy should be very smooth with bits of giblet and turkey swimming in it.
- I use a small whisk to make gravy...the key is to keep stirring. Don't even think of leaving it alone for a minute.
- Another key to making good gravy is to roast the pan in an old fashioned pan that the meat will stick to, so that you have bits of skin and turkey in the gravy. The object is a gravy that is pure delicious turkey flavor.

66. Madras Goat Chili With Cucumber Raita

Serving: Serves 4-6 | Prep: | Cook: | Ready in:

Ingredients

- Madras Goat Chili
- 1 pound ground goat meat
- 1 medium onion, chopped
- 1 15 oz. can coconut milk
- 1 15 oz. can diced tomatoes
- 1 15 oz can chickpeas, drained and rinsed
- 3 tablespoons madras curry paste
- 1/4-1/2 teaspoons chili powder
- Pinch salt
- 2 tablespoons rice bran, peanut, or vegetable oil
- 2 tablespoons chopped cilantro
- 3 tablespoons chopped scallions, greens only
- cooked rice or pita bread, to serve
- Cucumber Raita
- 1.5 cups thick, Greek-style yogurt
- 1/2 medium cucumber, peeled, seeded, and finely diced
- 1 tablespoon finely minced red onion
- 1 teaspoon ground cumin
- 1/2 teaspoon lemon juice
- salt & pepper to taste

Direction

- Madras Goat Chili
- Brown the goat meat in a heavy skillet. Drain and set aside.
- Heat the oil in a Dutch oven over medium heat. Add the onions and sauté until soft, about 10 minutes.
- Raise the heat to medium-high. Add the goat meat, diced tomatoes, coconut milk, chickpeas, curry paste, chili powder (1/4 to 1/2 tsp, depending on preference), and salt to the onions. Stir well to combine. Bring to a boil then reduce to a simmer. Simmer for 45 minutes uncovered, stirring every once in a while.
- Meanwhile make the raita.

- Cucumber Raita
- Using a fork, mix together all of the ingredients in a medium bowl, mashing the cucumber a bit. Let sit 20-30 minutes in the refrigerator while the chili cooks. Taste and adjust the seasonings.
- Once the 45 minutes is up, remove the chili from the heat and stir in the cilantro and scallions. Taste and adjust the seasonings as needed.
- Serve atop rice or with pita bread. Place a dollop of raita atop each serving.

67. Madras Goat Curry

Serving: Serves 4 | Prep: | Cook: | Ready in:

Ingredients

- 1 pound boneless goat stew meat
- 3 tablespoons canola oil
- 1 small onion, thinly sliced
- 1 15oz can diced tomatoes, drained
- 1 15oz can coconut milk
- 3-4 tablespoons Madras curry paste (depending on preference)
- pinch red pepper flakes
- salt
- rice or pita bread, to serve

Direction

- In a heavy-bottomed Dutch oven heat 2 tbsp. oil over medium-high heat. Add the stew meat in batches, making sure not to crowd the pan, turning until browned on all sides. After each batch remove to a waiting plate and continue until all the meat has been browned.
- Add the remaining 1 tbsp. oil and sauté the onions until soft and translucent, scraping up any browned bits that are stuck to the bottom of the pan.
- Add the stew meat back into the pot, followed by the tomatoes and coconut milk. Add the 3 tbsp. Madras curry paste (4 tbsp. if you prefer a stronger curry flavor), the chopped fresh cilantro, and salt & red pepper flakes to taste. Stir well to combine.
- Bring curry to a boil, reduce heat to low, cover, and cook 45 minutes – 1 hour, until the meat is tender. Taste halfway through and adjust seasonings.
- Serve hot on a bed of rice or with pita bread to mop up the curry sauce.

68. Maple Braised Rabbit And Carrots

Serving: Serves 4 | Prep: | Cook: | Ready in:

Ingredients

- 1 whole rabbit cut into 8 pieces
- 1 tablespoon whole white peppercorns
- 1 tablespoon whole black peppercorns
- 1 cinnamon stick
- 3 cups water plus 3 cups ice
- 1/3 cup kosher salt, plus 2 teaspoons more for the flour
- 1/3 cup sugar
- 3 cups ice
- 1 cup flour
- 1 teaspoon ground pepper
- 3 tablespoons butter
- 5 cloves garlic, chopped
- 2 large shallots, peeled and sliced
- 1 cup dry white wine
- 1 cup chicken stock
- 2 cups peeled carrot in 1/2-inch slices
- 1/4 cup grade B maple syrup
- 8 fresh sage leaves

Direction

- Is your rabbit cut up for you? If not, cut off the hoppers and the front legs (I do this with kitchen shears). Then remove the spine and portion the saddle into 4 pieces. There is a side flap that you can either leave loose (I do, I am

lazy) or use to create a roll that you can secure with a toothpick.
- Make the brine: Toast the peppercorns and cinnamon stick in a large saucepan for a few minutes until they are fragrant. Pour in the water, then add the salt and sugar. Bring it to a boil to dissolve the salt and sugar, then turn off the heat. Add the ice. Put the rabbit pieces in a large container and pour the cool brine over top. Refrigerate for several hours (this is a good morning task -- do the rest at dinner time)
- Heat the oven to 325° F. Get out your biggest oven-ready skillet (alternatively, you can brown in a skillet and then move the rabbit to a baking dish). Mix the flour with the 2 remaining teaspoons of salt and the ground pepper in a shallow dish. Remove the rabbit from the brine and try to get most of the peppercorns off. Pat it dry, then dredge each piece in flour. Melt the butter over medium-high heat and then place the rabbit pieces in the pan. Don't overcrowd them -- you will likely need to do this in batches. Brown each piece on both sides until golden brown, then remove from the pan.
- When all of the rabbit is browned, add the garlic and shallots to the pan and brown them for just a couple of minutes. Add the wine, then stock, and scrape all of the good stuff off the bottom of the pan. Allow this to simmer for 4 to 5 minutes.
- Now add the rabbit back in with the liquids. Toss the carrots and maple syrup together, then position them amongst the rabbit pieces. Add the sage leaves, hit it with a bit more pepper, then cover the pan with foil and bake for 30 minutes. After 30 minutes, remove the foil and bake for 30 more. Finish the rabbit by turning the oven to 375° F and cooking for 10 more minutes. Then remove it from the oven and allow it to rest while you take eleventy billion pictures. Remove the sage leaves before eating.
- That's all! Hippity, hoppity, dinner is ready!

69. Maple Glazed Magret De Canard (Duck Breasts)

Serving: Serves 2 | Prep: 0hours10mins | Cook: 0hours20mins | Ready in:

Ingredients

- 1 pound duck breast (either one large one, or two smaller ones)
- 2 pinches salt
- 2 pinches pepper
- 1/4 cup high-quality maple syrup
- 1/2 tablespoon soy sauce
- 1/2 tablespoon sweetened soy sauce (or add 1/4 tbsp sugar to 1/2 tbsp regular soy)
- 1 tablespoon balsamic vinegar

Direction

- Trim the duck breast(s) so that the fat is even with the meat all the way around. No extra fat should be hanging over the meat.
- Using a sharp blade, score the fat in diagonal lines in one direction, then rotate 90 degrees and score the fat in the other direction to create a cross-hatch pattern. Be sure not to cut into the meat, just into the fat layer. Season both sides with salt and pepper.
- If you are working with one large breast, pre-heat your oven to 400F. If you are working with two small breasts, you will finish them on the stovetop.
- Place the duck breast(s), skin side down, in a cold (oven-safe) pan over medium heat. As the fat renders, use a spoon to remove the excess (strain it through cheesecloth and save it; never let duck fat go to waste). Render until the skin is crispy and a dark golden brown. This may take 10-15 minutes.
- While the duck breasts are rendering, mix the maple syrup, balsamic vinegar, soy sauce, and sweet soy sauce in a small bowl. If you are adding sugar to regular soy sauce, warm the sauce slightly in the microwave (~30 seconds) to help dissolve the sugar.

- Flip the breast(s) over and cook for a minute or so. Then pour the sauce over the top.
- If you are working with one large breast, move the pan to the pre-heated oven and cook for another 6-7 minutes. With two small breasts, an additional 2-3 minutes on the stovetop should suffice. Cook to an internal temperature of 120-130F, depending on how rare you like your duck.

70. My Brother's Pecan Crusted Venison

Serving: Serves 4-6 | Prep: | Cook: | Ready in:

Ingredients

- 1.5 cups Finely chopped pecans
- 1.5 pounds Venison steak, blackstrap or ham/roast sliced
- 1/3 cup Olive oil
- 1/2 cup Good German mustard

Direction

- Take venison, whatever parts you want to use, and pound to 1/4" thickness in individual portion sizes. Slather both sides with mustard and let sit about 5 minutes.
- Put pecans on shallow plate or pie pan. Take one piece of venison at a time and dredge in pecans, pressing to make sure they stick. Out on cookie sheet I. Single layer and set aside.
- Take an 8-10" frying pan and heat 2 tablespoons of olive oil. When it shimmers, add venison. Cook only one piece at a time. Let cook 3-5 minutes on each side; don't overcook or let pecans burn.
- When done, remove from pan to cookie sheet lined with paper towel. Keep in oven on lowest setting until all of the venison has been cooked.

71. Old Fashioned Cornbread Stuffing

Serving: Makes 12x18 lasagna pan | Prep: | Cook: | Ready in:

Ingredients

- 2 loaves white bread
- 1 9x13 pan cornbread
- 2 Medium onions, chopped
- 5 stalks celery chopped
- 2 qts Turkey broth, made previously
- Dried Sage and poultry seasoning
- Salt & Pepper to taste
- 4 Eggs, slightly beaten
- Turkey Giblets

Direction

- Toast the bread and let set overnight. Cut bread into croutons.
- Prepare the cornbread and crumble. Let this set overnight to dry out.
- Add chopped onions and celery to turkey stock and simmer until tender.
- Add turkey stock to mixture of croutons and cornbread. Add sage, salt and pepper to taste. Add eggs and mix well.
- Place in greased pan and bake for 45 minutes to 1 hour. If the stuffing looks dry, pour more stock over and let it be absorbed.

72. Ostrich Stuffed Peppers

Serving: Serves 2 | Prep: | Cook: | Ready in:

Ingredients

- 2 peppers (red, yellow, orange)
- 1 pound ostrich
- 1/2 red onion
- 1 teaspoon cumin
- 1 serrano chili
- 2 dashes feta

- 1 splash coconut oil
- 1 splash olive oil
- 1 dash salt & pepper

Direction

- Preheat the oven to 400F.
- Start by cutting the peppers in half and removing the insides. Be careful not to puncture the pepper while doing this otherwise it will leak in the oven. For extra effect, leave the stalk in place, cutting it in half as you halve the pepper.
- In a skillet and with a little coconut oil, sauté the garlic, chili, cumin and onions until soft. Turn the heat up a little to medium-high, add the ostrich and fry until brown. Season with the salt and pepper.
- Remove the ostrich from the heat, lay the peppers on a roasting tray and spoon the ostrich into the peppers. Drizzle with a little olive oil before placing in the oven and roasting until the peppers are soft and juicy with the edges beginning to brown, about 25 - 30 mins.
- Optionally, crumble a little feta on top and garnish with fresh cilantro.

73. Pan Fried Duck Livers On Wholemeal Toast

Serving: Serves 1 | Prep: | Cook: | Ready in:

Ingredients

- 1 small red onion, finely sliced
- 2 French shallots, finely sliced
- 1 clove of garlic, finely chopped
- 2 tomatoes, de-seeded and finely chopped
- 12 ounces duck livers, trimmed and sliced thinly
- 4 tablespoons extra virgin olive oil
- 1/4 cup brandy (Armagnac if you have)
- 1 handful Italian flat leaf parsley, chopped
- soft green lettuce leaves for toast
- salt and pepper as desired

Direction

- On moderate heat, cook the onion and French shallots in the olive oil in a frying pan until they are soft and caramelizing. Stir periodically to ensure the mixture does not catch. Salt it to your taste. Add the garlic and continue the cooking process for another 4-5 minutes. Be careful not to brown them. Add the diced tomatoes and continue to cook until they are just beginning to soften. Remove from the pan into a bowl.
- Wipe the frying pan out with a paper towel. Add more olive oil. When the pan is medium hot, place the duck livers in to cook for about 2-minutes on each side. It is easy to dry the slices out so be prepared to move quickly if they are cooked on the outside and pink inside. They will continue to cook a bit after being taken from the pan.
- Turn up the heat under the pan and, when hot, pour in the brandy and ignite. When flame has died down stir any caught food from the bottom. When the brandy has almost cooked away, fold through the vegetables plus the handful of parsley and the chicken liver to quickly warm.
- Quickly toast 2 slices of whole meal slices of bread. When toasted, brush them lightly with extra virgin olive oil. Place the soft green lettuce leaves on the bread. Spoon the duck livers and vegetables on the toast. Dinner for 1 is served. The recipe can be multiplied to cater for the number dining. Smaller serves would make a delightful small starter to a meal.

74. Paperino V Pierino; Duck Ragu And Pappardelle, The Thrilla In L'Aquila

Serving: Serves 4 | Prep: | Cook: | Ready in:

Ingredients

- 1 1/2 pounds boneless duck breast with skin
- 1 medium red onion, chopped
- 1 carrot chopped in small dice
- 1 clove garlic, crushed and chopped
- 1 small branch rosemary (leaves stripped off and finely chopped)
- 3 -5 fresh sage leaves, roughly chopped
- 1/2 stick cinnamon
- 5 -6 juniper berries, about 1 tablespoon
- 5 whole cloves
- 8 black (or white) peppercorns
- 1 tablespoon balsamic vinegar (I use fig balsamic but that's a minor nuance)
- 1 tablespoon tomato paste (you buy it in the tube, right?)
- 1 splash Grand Marnier (optional)
- 1/2 cup dry red wine
- 1 cup poultry stock (ideally, duck stock but a brown chicken stock is fine)
- 1 tablespoon fresh grated orange zest
- 1 9-10 ounce package of pappardelle pasta (Rustichella d'Abruzzo brand highly preferred)
- Grated pecorino cheese

Direction

- Prepare your mise en place of onion, carrot and garlic
- In your cro-magnon mortar grind up the juniper, cinnamon, rosemary, peppercorns and cloves together. Or use a spice grinder. Just don't turn them into gun powder.
- Now address the duck. "Good afternoon, Paperino."
  "Ppphhwwwwaaaaapphqquaccccckkkkk, AFLAC"!
- Remove the skin and fat from the duck breasts. You can accomplish most of this bare knuckled but use a sharp knife to trim any stragglers. With that same sharp knife cut the meat into ¼" bits. They don't have to be totally uniform. DO NOT DISCARD THE SKIN!
- Heat up the heavy pot in which you will cook your ragù over medium flame. Place the skin pieces fat side down in the pot. Remain vigilant. Render as much fat as you can from the skin, working vigilantly. Duck fat has a low smoke point so don't let the skin pieces burn or you will have to discard the oil and start over, because your ragù will be very bitter if you fail to pay attention. When you think you have rendered as much fat as possible remove the skins and set aside. There should be a lot of fat here. Off heat ladle out all but about 2 tbsp. of that fat. But ladle that stuff into a jar or something and refrigerate. It's like holding a little bit of gold in your fridge. Great for frying potatoes in, so don't waste it.
- Return the pot to heat and add your mise. Season with salt and pepper as you go. Give it some color and push to the back of the pot. Add the duck and color that as well, but don't brown it or it will become way too chewy. Add the splash of Grand Marnier (if using) and let the alcohol cook off.
- Stir in the herbs and tomato paste and aromatize your kitchen. Let this cook for five minutes or so.
- Add the vinegar, followed by the wine. Add the stock. Taste for salt. Reduce to a simmer. Cover and allow to cook for up to two hours. This tends to be a wet sauce.
- Cook the pasta
- Zest the orange and add that to the ragù.
- Plate up the pasta. Top with a ladle of ragu and grating of pecorino on each individual plate.
- Notes to cook: I'm serious about not burning the skin. I've done it accidentally and now I don't. Pay attention to that. Please don't waste that wonderful duck fat. Also, I kind of like to toss at least one piece of that skin into the ragu as it simmers down, just amping up the duck flavor. You don't have to serve it, you can discard it like a bay leaf after, but you might want to consider the technique.
- ….the recommended pasta, "Rustichella d'Abruzzo" is the best dried pasta in all of Italy. Their extruded shapes are still made using bronze (as opposed to Teflon) dies. It's more expensive than Ronzoni or Barilla of

course but worth it. If you are an able hand at making pappardelle from scratch, by all means go at it. I do from time to time. But this is one of those cases where the pasta is so good that you shouldn't have to bother. Probably 90% of the ristoranti, trattorie, osterie in Italy use commercial pasta. I can name some that don't.

- Breading: as breading goes: a wash and some crunch. Here we used egg and crushed matzo coconut/soy work well w/rice flour
- Refrigerate till firm or freeze fry @375 (5-7min) until golden
- Dipping sauce: combine cream, mix, and paste; fold well

75. Pappas Relenas (R.F.U.G.) Chubby Spud

Serving: Serves 8-10 | Prep: | Cook: | Ready in:

Ingredients

- potato prep
- 5 pounds potato; peeled
- 4 teaspoons blk.pepper
- 1 tablespoon salt
- .25 cups milk
- 4 cups breading
- 2 cups wash
- filling and breading
- 2.5 pounds chorizo; out of casing
- 1 bunch cilantro; chopped
- 1 shallot; diced
- 1 galic; diced
- 1 carrot; diced
- 1 celery; diced
- 1 cup don't forget the cheese
- 2 pints sour cream
- 1 packet onion soup mix
- 4 tablespoons ancho paste

Direction

- Boil potatoes 20 min. (till you can break), toss w/ seasoning and milk; I say toss, we're not making mashed. Cool to workable.
- Brown meat, add seasonings; sauté lightly set aside when cool mix in cheese.
- With measuring tablespoon as form, press out ten; taking two, indent using thumb (2 football halves) use 2tsp filling and form (football) (~)

76. Passion Fruit Muffins

Serving: Makes 6 | Prep: | Cook: | Ready in:

Ingredients

- 2.5 Passion Fruit
- 1 Egg
- 1 tablespoon sugar (about 50 grams)
- 0.5 pounds Quark
- 1 tablespoon Pastry Flour
- liquid sweetener (to taste)
- 2 Mixed Berries

Direction

- Cut the passion fruits in half and scoop out flesh with a spoon. Put flesh of 1 passion fruit in a small bowl and reserve. Place remaining pulp in another bowl.
- Separate the eggs. Beat egg whites in a tall vessel with a hand mixer until stiff, then gradually add 2/3 of the sugar while beating.
- Gently fold the egg whites into the batter with a whisk and add sweetener to taste.
- Place baking cups in the muffin tin, pour in the batter and gently smooth. Bake in preheated oven at 180°C (fan 160°C, gas: mark 2-3) (approximately 350 ° F) until golden brown, 20-25 minutes. Let cool completely in the tin on a wire rack.
- Rinse berries, drain and cut into small pieces if necessary. Mix with reserved passion fruit pulp. Spoon over the muffins and serve.

77. Paul Virant's Make Ahead Roasted Turkey With Smothered Gravy

Serving: Serves 6 to 8 | Prep: | Cook: | Ready in:

Ingredients

- To break down the turkey and make the stock:
- One 15-pound turkey
- Turkey backbone, neck and wings (from above)
- 2 onions, roughly chopped
- 2 carrots, roughly chopped
- 2 stalks celery, roughly chopped
- 1 gallon water
- 4 sprigs thyme
- 2 bay leaves
- 5 black peppercorns
- To brine and roast the breast and braise the legs ahead (and finish day-of):
- 2 tablespoons grapeseed or other neutral oil
- Turkey drumsticks and thighs (from above)
- Kosher salt and freshly ground black pepper, to season
- Gizzards (from above, optional)
- 1 onion, roughly chopped
- 1 carrot, roughly chopped
- 2 stalks celery, roughly chopped
- 5 to 7 cloves garlic, roughly chopped
- 1 cup white wine
- 8 cups turkey stock (from above)
- 1 gallon water
- 1/2 cup kosher salt
- 1/2 cup packed dark brown sugar
- 1/4 cup Herbes de Provence
- 2 heads garlic, halved crosswise (but left unpeeled)
- 1 onion, sliced
- Bone-in, skin-on turkey breasts (from above)
- 1/2 cup + 2 tablespoons unsalted butter, divided
- 1/2 cup all-purpose flour
- 2 cups whole milk

Direction

- To break down the turkey and make the stock:
- Butcher the turkey (or ask your butcher to do it — as early as Sunday): Cut away the wings from the breasts and reserve for the broth. Remove the gizzards and save for the Smothered Gravy. Remove the heart and liver from the cavity and discard or reserve for another use (Virant puts his in his stuffing).
- With the bird breast side up on the cutting board, remove the legs with a sharp boning knife: make a cut in between the breast and thigh joint, and then sever the connection between the thigh and the back. Once both legs have been removed, detach the thighs from the drumsticks, then cover tightly with plastic wrap and refrigerate. With sturdy knife or pair of kitchen shears, cut out the backbone and neck, leaving the breast meat on the breastbone. (When propped breast-side-up, the turkey will look ready to roast, just without legs.) Reserve the backbone and neck for the stock and refrigerate the breast meat tightly covered in plastic wrap until ready to brine.
- Make the stock (as early as Sunday — you'll need about 4 hours of inactive time): Heat the oven to 400° F. Place the backbone, neck, and wings in a roasting pan and roast until the skin and bones begin to brown, about 15 minutes. Add the onions, carrots, and celery and roast until the vegetables have caramelized, about 15 minutes more. Scrape the bones and vegetables into a stockpot and cover with about 1 gallon of water. Deglaze the roasting pan with a splash of water and scrape the caramelized bits into the pot. Add the thyme, bay leaves, and peppercorns and bring to a boil. Decrease to a gentle simmer and cook for 3 hours. Strain the stock through a fine-mesh strainer, cool, and refrigerate. Before using, scrape away any fat that has risen to the surface and reserve for your stuffing. Makes 16 cups stock, 8 cups for the Smothered Gravy, with extra to use in your stuffing or reserve for another use.
- To brine and roast the breast and braise the legs ahead (and finish day-of):

- Braise the drumsticks and thighs (Monday or Tuesday—you'll need about 2 1/2 to 3 hours inactive time): Heat the oven to 300° F. In a large sauté pan over high heat, heat the oil. Season the legs, thighs, and gizzards well with salt and pepper. In batches, sear the turkey pieces until well-browned all over (if they're sticking, just leave them a bit longer—they'll release once they get a good sear) and transfer to a large roasting pan. In the same sauté pan, sauté the onion, carrot, celery, and garlic until soft and lightly caramelized, about 6 minutes. Deglaze with the wine, scraping up the brown bits, and simmer to reduce the liquid by half. Spoon the stock and vegetables over the thighs and legs, cover the roasting pan with aluminum foil, and braise until the meat is very tender, about 2 hours. Cool the legs in the braising liquid and refrigerate overnight.
- Pull the drumstick and thigh meat (Wednesday or Thursday): Scrape off any fat that has risen to the top of the braising liquid and set aside to use in your (delicious) stuffing. Remove the legs and thighs from the braising liquid and pull the meat of the bones. Bring the liquid to a boil, then strain and set aside to make the gravy or cool and refrigerate until ready to make the gravy.
- Make the brine (up to a week ahead): In a large pot, bring the water, salt, sugar, herbs, garlic, and onion to a boil. Simmer until the salt and sugar have dissolved. Cool (in a water bath, if you're in a hurry) and refrigerate.
- Brine the breasts (Tuesday or Wednesday): Place the breasts in a large storage container or pot and cover with the chilled brine (the meat should be completely submerged). Cover and refrigerate for at least 1 but no more than 2 days.
- Roast the breasts (Wednesday or Thursday—you will need about 2 hours inactive time): Remove the breasts from the brine, pat dry, and let sit at room temperature for an hour. Heat the oven to 425° F. Melt 2 tablespoons of the butter, place the breasts in a roasting pan fitted with a rack, and brush the skin all over with melted butter. Roast until the meat reaches an internal temperature of 135° F to 140° F, about 45 minutes. (Note: This lower internal temperature helps prevent the meat from drying out—the meat will finish cooking through gently in the gravy when rewarming. If you're roasting on Thursday and would prefer to take it closer to 165° F and serve the gravy on the side, that is fine too.) Let the meat rest for about 15 minutes. Cool the breasts, cover, and refrigerate overnight.
- Make the gravy (ideally Thursday, but can be made Wednesday and rewarmed if needed): In a small saucepan, melt 1/2 cup of the butter. Stir in the flour and cook until the roux turns pale gold and smells slightly nutty, like browned butter. In a large pot, bring the reserved braising liquid and milk to a boil. Decrease to a simmer and whisk in the roux. Simmer over medium-low heat, stirring often, until the gravy coats the back of a spoon, about 15 minutes. Add the reserved drumstick and thigh meat and simmer until the meat is hot. Keep warm. If you need to make the gravy ahead and chill it, rewarm it in a heavy pot or saucepan over medium heat, whisking in extra stock as needed to thin to your preferred consistency. Take care not to let the bottom scorch.
- Warm and serve the breasts (Thursday): With a sharp knife, remove the whole breasts from the breast bone, then slice each breast crosswise in 1/2-inch slices. (If the breasts are still slightly pink, the hot gravy and warm oven will finish cooking the meat, while keeping it moist.) Place the slices in a large casserole and spoon the hot gravy over the top. Place the turkey in a warm oven (250° F) until ready to serve.

78. Pheasant Potpie

Serving: Serves 6 to 8 | Prep: | Cook: | Ready in:

Ingredients

- For the filling
- 1 tablespoon canola oil
- 1 1/4 pounds pheasant meat, cubed
- 1 cup ham lardons
- 1 cup yellow onion, minced
- 3 carrots, peeled and sliced
- 1 large potato, peeled and cubed
- 1 turnip peeled and cubed
- 2 celery stalks, chopped
- 3 tablespoons unsalted butter
- 3 tablespoons all purpose flour
- 1/2 cup green onion, chopped into thin rounds
- 3 cups water or vegetable stock
- 2 teaspoons fresh thyme, minced
- kosher salt and fresh ground black pepper
- For the topping:
- 2 cups fine grind 100% whole wheat flour
- 2 teaspoons sugar
- 2 teaspoons baking powder
- 1 teaspoon baking soda
- 1/2 teaspoon kosher salt
- 1/4 cup lard
- 1 cup whole milk yogurt or buttermilk

Direction

- Preheat the oven to 425? F. In an oven proof twelve inch skillet with two inch sides heat the oil over medium high heat. When the oil is hot enough to keep the meat from sticking add the pheasant and brown it. Once it has browned remove it from the pan to a plate. Drain the grease but don't wipe out the pan.
- Place the pan back over the heat and reduce it to medium. Add the ham and render it till soft-crispy. Add the butter, yellow onion, carrot, turnips and potatoes. Season it with a healthy pinch of salt and some pepper. Cook until the onions are starting to become tender.
- Add the flour and stir it to get it to combine with the melted butter. Add the thyme, green onions and water or stock. Bring the stock to a boil while stirring. Stirring keeps the roux from lumping so stir until you are boiling. Taste and adjust the seasoning
- Reduce the heat to a simmer.
- In a mixing bowl combine the flour, sugar, baking soda and powder and the salt.
- Using your hands break the lard up into the flour then rub your hands together like you are warming them. Do this until you have a mealy looking flour mixture.
- Add the yogurt or buttermilk to the flour and stir with as few strokes as possible to bring the dough together, in other words try not to develop a lot of gluten.
- Remove the stew from the heat and stir in the browned pheasant.
- Using large table or soup spoons scoop up balls of dough and place them onto the top of the stew. Make sure to spread them out evenly. They may look far apart but they will swell up in the oven.
- Bake the potpie in the oven until the biscuits are brown and the stew is bubbly. About 15 to 20 minutes.
- Let cool a few minutes, it is thermonuclear, then serve.

79. Pizza With Ducks Breast, Goat Cheese, Greens And Figs

Serving: Makes 4 | Prep: | Cook: | Ready in:

Ingredients

- Onion confit
- 3 medium onions
- 1 tablespoon sugar
- 1/4 cup olive oil
- 1 tablespoon white wine vinegar
- Pizza
- 4 pieces pizza dough (small)
- 2 tablespoons olive oil
- 1 cup fresh goat cheese, crumbled
- 2 cups arugula
- 3 cups watercress
- 6 fgis, cut into slices
- 1 handful walnuts, coarsed
- 2 tablespoons honey

Direction

- For the onion confit, cut the onions into thin slices. Heat the olive oil in a cast iron (medium-high heat), add the onions and sugar, season with salt and pepper. Cook the onions until golden and soften, about 8-10 minutes. Add 1 tbsp. white wine vinegar and reduce to medium heat and cook for another 5 minutes
- Preheat oven to 450F. Place the pizza stone or oven tray on a lower rack.
- On a floured surface, roll out your dough into four circles (23 cm). Place the dough on the pizza stone or the oven tray covered with parchment paper. Brush the pizzas with olive oil. Spread out the onion confit on the dough than sprinkle with goat cheese.
- Bake the pizza for 12 minutes, until golden. Take out of the oven and garnish with the watercress, arugula, duck, figs and walnuts. Season to taste and sprinkle with honey. Serve warm

80. Pomegranate Gastrique (Sauce)

Serving: Makes 1-2 cups | Prep: | Cook: |Ready in:

Ingredients

- Pomegranates
- 1 tablespoon Sugar
- 1 to 1 1/2 Pomegranates
- Pinch salt
- Beef Broth: Roasted bones and veggies seasoned with salt & pepper. Then you take them out of the 400 oven, put in small stock pot, add water and cook for hours.
- 1 cup Good quality beef broth
- 1/2 cup Fresh Pomegranate juice
- 1 cup cooked Pomegranate seeds
- Salt & Pepper
- 1 Bay Leaf
- 1 splash Good Balsamic Vinegar
- 1 -2 tablespoons Red Currant Jam
- 1-2 teaspoons Lingonberry preserve (optional)

Direction

- Divide the Pomegranates and take out all the juicy seeds. Do this over a colander to get out as much juice as possible. Squeeze with back of a wooden spoon and then turn them over into a small pot, add a pinch of salt and a tablespoon on sugar. Cook a few minutes until more juices come out. Strain the liquid and keep the seeds and juice separate. Set aside.
- Warm up broth and reduce, add Pomegranate juice, about 1 cup of the red seeds and S&P, Bay Leaf, splash of Balsamic Vinegar, Lingo berry jam or Currant Jelly. Cook till you like consistency. Use or freeze for later.
- PS. I took 2 Cornish Game hens, sprinkled them with S&P on the inside and seasoned salt on the outside. In the cavity I divided a clementine and shoved it in. I basted with the above sauce a few times in a 350 oven till they were done. (Maybe an hour) Major hit at my house with roasted veggies and salad.

81. Portmanteau'd Lamb Chops

Serving: Serves 4 | Prep: | Cook: |Ready in:

Ingredients

- 4 Large Lamb Loin Chops, 4-5cm thick
- 2 Chicken Livers, about 25 g
- 6 Medium size Shiitake or Porcini Mushrooms
- 100 grams Butter
- 2 Eggs, beaten
- 250 grams White Breadcrumbs
- Salt and Pepper

Direction

- Preparation Time: ~40min | Cooking Time: ~15min | Pre-Heat Oven: 400
- Remove the skin and trim some of the fat from each chop. Using a very sharp knife, slit the

lean eye of the chop, cutting in-wards toward the bone. Set aside.
- Finely chop the livers and mushrooms. Season to taste with salt and pepper. Melt half of the butter in a small frying pan. Add the mushroom and liver mixture, and cook gently for about 5 minutes without browning.
- Allow the liver and mushroom mixture to cool. Once cooled, stuff the mixture in the incisions made in the chops.
- Optional: Sew the chop shut to keep the stuffing in during cooking. However, if you are careful, you can avoid the stuffing spilling out without sewing shut.
- Dip the stuffed chops in the beaten eggs and coat generously with breadcrumbs. Place the chops in a roasting tray
- Melt the remaining butter over low heat and pour a little over each of the chops.
- Bake in the pre-heated oven for 7 minutes, then flip and bake for another 7 minutes. This will result in a medium rare chop.
- Allow the chops to rest for a few minutes before you cut into them.
- If you sewed the chops shut, remember to remove the stitches before plating.

82. RABBIT PAELLA

Serving: Serves 6 | Prep: | Cook: | Ready in:

Ingredients

- 2 1/2 pound rabbit, cut into small (3-4 inch) pieces
- 1 1/2 cups rice (paella rice such as bomba)
- 8 ounces pork chorizo, casing removed
- 3 cups wild mushrooms, 1 c ea baby shitake, oyster and hen of the woods (or your favorites)
- 3 1/2 cups chicken broth
- 1 cup yellow onion, small dice
- 6 ounces dry red wine (syrah, cab franc)
- 2 tablespoons olive oil
- 1 cup toasted walnuts
- 2 anchovies (oil packed)
- 3 tablespoons parsley leaves, chopped
- a pinch of saffron
- pitted green olives
- salt and black pepper to taste
- ******4 duck confit legs (OPTIONAL)

Direction

- Put 2 tablespoons olive oil in a paella pan and the rabbit pieces and brown well on all sides. Put a few turns of black pepper on the rabbit as it cooks. Remove and set aside.
- Add the onions to the pan.
- Remove the casings from the pork chorizo, discard the casings and roll the pork into small meatballs about one inch in diameter and add to the onions in the pan. Roll the balls around the pan to release more fat and brown them.
- After a few minutes add the mushrooms.
- While the onions, mushrooms and the balls are cooking, make a pesto with 1/2 the toasted walnuts, chopped parsley, saffron and anchovies using a mortar and pestle. Add a little broth to get a proper consistency.
- Deglaze the pan with the wine...a couple of minutes.
- Add the pesto and the rest of the walnuts to the pan and spread all the ingredients evenly around the pan.
- Add the rice and the broth to the pan. After you spread the rice evenly around the pan and add the broth, do not stir.
- Add the browned rabbit back to the pan. Add the duck confit if you have it already made or if you find it at your grocery deli.
- Put the paella in a 375 degree oven for about 30 minutes. Do not open and stir the rice.
- Remove from the oven and leave on the counter for 10 minutes. (It will continue to cook during this time) DO NOT cover the pan with a lid...it will steam the rice and it will not be crispy!
- Add the olives.
- ***To make the recipe quick and easy, read the recipe first and then make the pork chorizo

meatballs and the pesto ahead of time and have all other ingredients ready to go!
- OPTIONAL: For a dinner party, I added 4 duck confit legs. I really like the extra flavor and often keep a crock of duck confit in my cooler.

83. Rabbit Braised In Sour Cream And Horseradish Sauce

Serving: Serves 3-6 | Prep: | Cook: |Ready in:

Ingredients

- • 1 Rabbit (4 Pounds, cut in 6 portions)
- • 2 medium shallots (diced)
- • 4 cloves garlic (minced)
- • 3 tablespoons olive oil
- • Salt, fresh ground black pepper
- • 1 tablespoon all purpose flour
- • 1 tablespoon whitevine or champagne vinegar
- • 2 cups chicken stock
- • 1 ½ cups sour cream
- • 2 tablespoons fresh Horseradish (grinded)
- • 2 teaspoons fresh thyme.

Direction

- Heat a large nonstick skillet over medium heat. Preheat oven to 325 degrees F.
- 1. Clean, wash and cut the Rabbit first along the spine then in 6 portions (3 from each side).
- 2. Dry each portion with paper towel
- 3. Salt and pepper both sides.
- 4. Add 3 tablespoons olive oil to the skillet.
- 5. Brown the rabbit parts evenly on both sides.
- 6. Transfer to a Dutch oven or heavy pot.
- 7. In the same skillet, on medium flame sauté shallots and horseradish, then in about 10 minutes add garlic and cook another minute
- 8. Stir in the vinegar.
- 9. Mix in flour and cook constantly stirring.
- 10. When the flour is completely absorbed add slowly hot chicken stock.
- 11. With a wooden spoon scrape all the brown bits from the bottom of the skillet.
- 12. Cook until thickened, add sour cream, thyme and bring to a simmer, Taste to adjust the seasonings.
- 13. Pour the sauce over the rabbit, cover the pot, and transfer to oven.
- 14. Cook for one hour or as long as needed for the meat to be very soft.
- Serve over rice or buttered noodles. It is also very tasty over sour cream mashed potatoes or roasted vegetables. Garnish with chopped herbs and green peas (quickly sautéed in a little butter and lemon juice).

84. Rabbit Porchetta

Serving: Serves 6 | Prep: | Cook: |Ready in:

Ingredients

- 1 large stewer rabbit, 4 to 6 pounds
- sea salt
- 4 cloves of garlic pounded to a fine paste in a mortar and pestle
- freshly ground black pepper
- 1 tablespoon fennel pollen
- zest of 2 lemons
- 1/2 cup chopped herbs, such as rosemary, oregano, parsley and sage
- 2 tablespoons extra virgin olive oil

Direction

- Bone the rabbit. Lay the rabbit on its back and check its abdominal cavity for kidneys or livers (they are often left attached). If either is present, remove them with a sharp knife and set aside. Remove the forelegs by using your hands to gently pry them away from the body. Then cut them off completely by following the natural seam under the foreleg. Reserve the forelegs for another use. Starting at the neck end, working with your boning knife against the rib cage, remove the meat from the bone.

When you reach the loin area, curve the tip of your knife around the loin until you hit the backbone. Repeat this process down the length of the rib cage until you reach the back legs. Remove the backbone by severing the tip of each vertebra while simultaneously pulling the rib cage away from the rabbit. Take care not to pierce through the meat. Separate the leg bones from the hip socket by gently popping them out of the socket from behind. Remove the bones from the legs on both sides, taking care to only cut as deep as the bone.

- Lay the completely boneless rabbit out on your work surface and rub the inside with the pounded garlic and lemon zest. Season both the inside and outside of the rabbit with the salt, pepper and fennel pollen then sprinkle the chopped herbs over the interior. Roll the boneless rabbit tightly around itself lengthwise. Tie with butcher's twine at 3-inch (7.5 cm) intervals. Wrap tightly with plastic wrap and refrigerate for one to three days.
- Preheat the oven to 425°F (220°C). Place the roulade on a rack fitted onto a roasting pan and lightly rub olive oil all over. Roast for about 45 minutes or until a meat thermometer registers 140°F (60°C) when inserted into the thickest portion of the roast. Remove from the oven and allow the roast to rest for 10 minutes before slicing into half-inch (1.25 cm) thick rounds. Strain the pan juices and spoon over the sliced meat.

85. Rabbit Sinatra Burgundy Style Rabbit, My Way (Warning: You May Also Make This With Chicken)

Serving: Makes 4-6 servings | Prep: | Cook: | Ready in:

Ingredients

- 6 ounces red onion finely chopped
- 6 ounces green bell pepper finely chopped
- 6 ounces celery finely chopped
- 1 or 2 small hot peppers, seeded, deveined and finely chopped
- 2 cloves garlic, finely chopped
- 1 3-pound (fresh) rabbit cut into 6 pieces
- 3/4 cup all purpose flour
- 2 1/2 teaspoons sea salt
- 3/4 teaspoon freshly ground black pepper
- 1/4 teaspoon cayenne
- 1/4 teaspoon ground mace
- 1 cup chicken stock
- 1/2 cup Dijon mustard
- 1 teaspoon crushed brown mustard seed
- 2 cups red wine (such as Côtes du Rhône)
- 1 cup water
- 1/4 teaspoon crushed red pepper flakes
- 1 teaspoon sea salt
- 1/4 cup Cognac
- 1 basket pearl onions

Direction

- Dredge rabbit pieces in flour mixture. Heat the olive oil in a deep-sided sauté pan. Sear rabbit on all sides to brown very well. Remove from pan and keep warm.
- Sauté vegetables in the same oil until soft.
- Blend the mustard and crushed seeds into the chicken stock. Add all the liquid to the pan. Add the salt and crushed red pepper. Return the rabbit to the pan. Cover tightly and allow to braise for 1 hour, or until very tender.
- Remove rabbit from pan. Raise heat and cook liquid down to one half. Purée vegetables in sauce with a stick blender or in a food processor fitted with the metal blade.
- Return sauce to pan and add 1/4 cup Cognac. Add 1 basket of pearl onions (peeled and trimmed) and allow to simmer for about 10 minutes, or until onions are tender. Return rabbit pieces to sauce to reheat and coat well with the sauce.
- Teacher's Tip: Serve with buttered noodles or mashed potatoes to sop up all the delicious sauce and a lovely Pommard wine.

86. Rabbit Stew À La Rainier

Serving: Serves 4 | Prep: | Cook: | Ready in:

Ingredients

- For the Marinade:
- 1 whole rabbit, cleaned and cut into 4 equally sized pieces
- 4 garlic cloves, peeled and smashed
- 2 teaspoons Herbes de Provence
- 2 cups dry vermouth
- For the Stew:
- 4 slices bacon, sliced crosswise in 1" pieces
- 1 bulb fennel, thinly sliced
- 2 branches of thyme
- salt & pepper
- 10 ounces canned tomatoes, chopped
- 1/2 pound small potatoes, sliced in half
- 8 cups best-quality meat stock

Direction

- For the Marinade:
- Marinate the rabbit with the vermouth, 4 cloves of peeled and smashed garlic, and the Herbes de Provence overnight in the fridge, turning occasionally.
- For the Stew:
- Choose a heavy pot large enough to hold the rabbit. Cook the bacon in the pot over medium high heat until the bacon just begins to brown. Transfer the bacon to a plate.
- Turn down the heat to medium, add the fennel, thyme, and 4 cloves of peeled and smashed garlic. Cook until the fennel softens and begins to brown.
- Set aside the vegetables with the bacon. Drain the rabbit, discarding the garlic from the marinade. Salt and pepper the meat. Turn the heat back up to medium high, and brown the rabbit. Cook until the rabbit skin is golden, approximately 10 minutes per side. Let the meat sit in the pan undisturbed for at least 5 minutes. Once the skin is browned it won't stick to the pan.
- Once the rabbit is browned, return the vegetables to the pot. Add the tomatoes (without their liquid), the potatoes (sliced in half), and the stock. Bring the stew to a boil, then partially cover the pot and let it simmer for two hours over medium-low heat.
- Serve at once with crusty bread for dipping, or keep the stew in the fridge for a day or three.

87. Rabbit With White Wine And Rosemary

Serving: Serves 4-6 | Prep: | Cook: | Ready in:

Ingredients

- 1 whole rabbit
- 1/4 cup white wine
- 1 dash white wine vinegar
- 1/8 cup olive oil
- 1 clove garlic
- 1 sprig rosemary
- Salt and pepper
- Optional: crushed red pepper
- Optional: 1 cup flour

Direction

- Cut the rabbit into pieces with a large butcher knife.
- If you like a creamier texture, place the flour into a shallow bowl and dust each piece of rabbit in flour on all sides. However, you can omit the flour if you wish. We like rabbit both ways.
- Mince the garlic and sauté it in the oil in a large pan until golden brown.
- Add the white wine and white wine vinegar, and allow the mixture to continue to simmer on medium heat.
- Carefully arrange the rabbit in the skillet.
- Add rosemary leaves, and salt and pepper to taste.
- If you like white meats with a little heat, add a little crushed red pepper.

- Cover, and cook over medium heat, turning on occasion, for approximately 20-25 minutes.
- Serve with vegetables or roasted potatoes.

88. Rabbit À La Moutarde

Serving: Serves four | Prep: | Cook: |Ready in:

Ingredients

- 3 to 4 pounds rabbit, cut into serving pieces
- Coarse salt
- 4 tablespoons (½ stick) unsalted butter
- 2 garlic cloves, peeled and finely minced
- 1 tablespoon Herbes de Provence
- 1 teaspoon teaspoon dried thyme
- 1 cup white wine
- 1 cup heavy cream
- ¼ cups smooth Dijon mustard
- 3 tablespoons whole-grain mustard
- 1 pound small potatoes, boiled until tender and halved

Direction

- Pat the rabbit pieces dry with paper towels and season aggressively with salt.
- Melt the butter in a large, heavy pot over medium-high heat. Add the rabbit pieces and cook, turning only once, until browned, about 5 minutes per side. Transfer the rabbit pieces to a plate and set aside.
- Add the shallots and garlic to the pot and cook, stirring occasionally, until just beginning to soften, about 5 minutes. Add the herbes de Provence, thyme, and wine to the pot and bring the mixture to a boil. Whisk in the cream and both of the mustards, then lower the heat and allow the mixture to simmer so that all of the flavors combine, just a minute or two. Season the mixture to taste with salt.
- Return the browned rabbit pieces to the pot and simmer, uncovered, until the rabbit is tender, about 20 minutes. Add the cooked potatoes during the last 10 minutes of cooking just to heat them through. Serve hot.

89. Rhonda's Chicken Liver Pate

Serving: Makes enough for a party (approximately 3 cups) | Prep: | Cook: |Ready in:

Ingredients

- Marinate the Chicken Livers
- 1 pound chicken livers, well-cleaned
- dry sherry (or liquor of choice), to cover
- Pate
- 1/2 cup unsalted butter, divided
- 8 ounces button or cremini mushrooms, sliced
- 1/2 cup sweet onion, diced
- 1 teaspoon kosher salt
- 1/2 teaspoon freshly ground black pepper
- 1/4 teaspoon turmeric
- 1/4 teaspoon sweet paprika
- 1/4 teaspoon freshly grated nutmeg
- 1/3 cup dry sherry

Direction

- Several hours or the night before you want to make the pate, pour over dry sherry to cover the chicken livers and allow to marinate in the refrigerator.
- Once livers have marinated, discard the sherry and dry the livers a bit by pouring into a strainer and giving it a good shake over the sink.
- In a large skillet, melt 3 tablespoons of butter over medium-high heat. Add the mushrooms and onions and sauté till soft, about 7 minutes.
- Add chicken livers and seasonings (salt, pepper, turmeric, paprika and nutmeg) and sauté 10 minutes or till cooked through.
- Scrape everything into a blender and allow to cool a bit. Meanwhile, turn up the heat under the skillet and deglaze the pan with 1/3 cup of sherry. Add this to blender, too.

- Add remaining 5 Tablespoons of butter to the mixture and secure blender lid (I hold a dishcloth in my hand and keep that hand on the lid - just in case!)
- Puree mixture till very smooth, adding a bit more butter or sherry, as needed.
- Pour mixture into a pretty serving dish, cover with plastic wrap and allow to cool and set in the fridge.
- Serve with crackers, toasted baguette slices, gherkin pickles, chopped onion, etc. If you want to make canapés, the pate can be put into a pastry bag and piped onto toast rounds or endive leaves. It's especially tasty piped into pitted dates.
- To make my most recent version of this pate, substitute dry rose wine for the sherry and use 1 1/2 lbs chicken livers, skipping the mushrooms. Also add the zest of one lemon and 1 Tablespoon minced fresh dill to the mixture in the blender, omitting the turmeric, paprika and nutmeg in the recipe.

90. Roast Duck With Vegetables

Serving: Serves 4 | Prep: | Cook: | Ready in:

Ingredients

- 1 duck (about 2kg)
- 3 teaspoons salt
- 1 teaspoon ground black pepper
- 1 teaspoon ground garlic
- 1 teaspoon red paprika
- 3 onions
- 4 cloves garlic
- 3 carrots
- 1 apple
- 1 orange
- 1 red bell pepper
- 2 bay leaves
- 200 milliliters stock (vegetable or chicken)
- 100 milliliters dry white wine

Direction

- The night before give the duck a good wash and then dry it with paper towels.
- Prepare seasoning: in a small bowl put 3 teaspoons salt, 1 tsp ground black pepper, 1 tsp ground dry garlic, 1 tsp red paprika and mix well.
- Gently rub the seasoning into the duck skin, covering every inch. Then, with a fork, poke a few holes into the breast skin (this will help air circulate and make the skin crisp).
- Roughly chop an onion and a few garlic cloves, and place it under the duck in a bowl. Cover the duck and set in the fridge overnight.
- The next day, preheat oven to 180°C. Get the duck out of the fridge, remove the cover and place duck onto a baking tray. Chop the remaining vegetables, the apple and orange into large chunks and place around the duck, add bay leaves and pour a dash of white wine and some stock over the bird and vegetables. Place the duck into the preheated oven to bake for about 2,5 - 3 hours.
- While the bird is roasting, make sure to keep it moist by pouring over the juices from the baking tray every 15 minutes or so. Roast the bird until the skin is golden brown and crispy.

91. Roast Gravy

Serving: Makes 2 quart | Prep: | Cook: | Ready in:

Ingredients

- Roast Chicken Stock
- 2 whole chickens
- Kosher salt
- Coarse ground black pepper
- 1 small yellow onion
- 2 ribs celery
- 2 carrots
- Roast Gravy
- Up to 1/2 cup (1 stick) butter
- Turkey giblets, neck and "Pope's nose"

- Kosher salt
- Coarse ground pepper
- 1 large yellow onion
- 1 stalk celery, well rinsed
- 2 whole carrots
- 2 quarts chicken stock, thawed if frozen
- Cornstarch
- Pan drippings
- All-purpose flour

Direction

- Roast Chicken Stock
- Up to a month before Thanksgiving: Remove giblets and neck from chicken and refrigerate. Rinse chicken and place in a roasting pan with a two-quart or more capacity. Sprinkle the chicken with 2 teaspoons of salt and a half teaspoon of pepper. Roast or bake as desired. Remove the meat from the breasts, legs and thighs and use in salads, sandwiches or entrees.
- Break the carcasses into pieces at the joints and place the pieces back in the roasting pan with the giblets and neck. Trim the ends from the onion, celery and carrot. Cut each vegetable into fourths, strew the pieces over the carcass, sprinkle with a teaspoon of salt and roast at 400 degrees for at least an hour, until you see lots of dark golden-amber coloring and can smell the umami.
- Remove pan from the oven and set it on the stove. Carefully pour two quarts (eight cups) of simmering water into the roasting pan, sprinkle with two teaspoons of salt and a quarter-teaspoon of pepper and give everything a gentle stir. Allow to rest until cool enough to handle. Strain the stock through a sieve lined with cheesecloth into a storage container. Freeze until needed. (If you need additional stock to moisten a stuffing or dressing, double the recipe but freeze in separate containers.)
- Roast Gravy
- With the butter, grease the bottom and sides of a 4-qt. Dutch oven or other oven-safe vessel. Use a tablespoon if you're roasting the turkey indoors and will have pan drippings; use the whole stick if you will be cooking your turkey in a way that drippings will not be collected. Add the turkey parts and sprinkle with a teaspoon of salt and a quarter-teaspoon of pepper. Trim the ends from the onion (do not peel it), cut it into eighths and put it in the pot. Trim two inches from the bottom and three inches from the top of the stalk of celery; put the trimmings, leaves and all, in the pot. Trim the ends from the carrots (do not peel), cut them into 1" pieces and place them in the pot. Put the pot into the oven set at 400 degrees and roast until most of the contents are caramelized, at least one-and-a-half hours (longer if the oven is being shared with something cooking at a lower temperature), stirring the contents once or twice.
- Remove the pot from the oven and place it on the stovetop. If any liquid remains in the bottom of the pot, cook it uncovered over low heat so that it doesn't sputter and pop on you. If only fat is in the bottom of the pot, allow it to cool down somewhat, then carefully pour or ladle the fat into a glass measuring cup. Pour the chicken stock over the roasted meat and vegetables and simmer for 1/2 hour.
- Make a slurry of 1/4 cup cornstarch and 3/4 cup water. Set aside.
- When your oven-roasted turkey is done, remove it from the pan to a carving board or cookie sheet to rest before slicing it. If there is a lot of liquid in the pan, cook it off on the stovetop so that all that's left in the roasting pan is lovely, gooey, sticky fond with clear turkey fat oozing over and through it. Add this fat to the fat in the measuring cup. If you have less than one cup of fat, add enough butter to bring it up to that level. Pour it back into the roasting pan. Stir in 3/4 cup flour and allow it to absorb the fat. Place the roasting pan over a low flame and let this roux cook for a full minute. Ladle in all the stock and half of the cornstarch slurry; turn the heat to medium and bring the gravy to a gentle boil, stirring constantly and scraping up the fond, for about three minutes. Adjust the consistency of the

gravy by adding more of the cornstarch slurry if it's too thin or water if it's too thick, and keep in mind that the gravy will thicken as it cools. Taste; add salt a quarter-teaspoon at a time if needed, and pepper.

92. Roasted Beets Paired With Duck Hearts

Serving: Serves 4-6 as an appetizer | Prep: | Cook: | Ready in:

Ingredients

- Roasted Beets
- 8 small chioggia beets and their tops
- 2 oranges
- 1 lemon
- 1 small bunch of thyme
- 1 head of garlic, split in two
- Salt
- Pepper
- Olive oil
- 1 shallot, minced
- Duck Hearts
- 12 duck hearts
- 2 tablespoons salt
- 1 tablespoon black pepper
- 1 tablespoon ground and toasted fennel seed
- 1 tablespoon brown sugar

Direction

- Remove the beet tops. Wash the beets well and leave one aside. In a hotel pan or casserole pan, dress the beets in the juice of one orange, plenty of salt, the garlic, thyme, salt, pepper and olive oil. Cover with tin foil and roast in the oven at 400 degrees. After 40 minutes, stick a knife into a beet to see if they are done. They should be, but sometimes beets can take forever. Adjust accordingly.
- When they are done, remove them from the oven and peel off the skins while they are still hot (if you let the beets cool, it will be a lot harder to remove the skin). Cut the beets into slices and pour the pan juice over the beets. Let the beets cool.
- While the beets are cooking, wash and dry the leaves. Marinate them in the juice of one of one orange, the juice of the lemon, salt and olive oil. Set aside.
- Also while the beets are cooking. Make a mixture of the salt, pepper, sugar and fennel. Toss the hearts in the salt mixture and set aside for an hour. After an hour, rinse the cure off the hearts and dry them. Skewer the hearts and grill each to medium rare (about 1.5 minutes on each side). Slice the hearts into quarters.
- Remove the beets from the liquid. Mince the marinated beet stems and combine with the beets and minced shallots. If it's a little dry, use some of the two marinating liquids. At the last minute, toss in the quartered duck hearts. Garnish with a pile of julienned raw Chioggia beet (no dressing).

93. Roasted And Whipped Bone Marrow

Serving: Makes about 1 cup | Prep: 0hours0mins | Cook: 1hours0mins | Ready in:

Ingredients

- 2 beef femur bones, canoed
- 1 tablespoon fresh parsley, minced
- 1 tablespoon fresh thyme, minced
- salt and pepper, to taste
- lemon wedges or white wine vinegar for serving

Direction

- Place canoed marrow bones, marrow side-up, on a roasting sheet lined with tinfoil and pre-heat your oven to 425° F. Roast for 25 minutes.
- When the bones have cooled enough to handle, scoop the marrow out into a bowl and

place it in the refrigerator to cool (Save your bones to make stock! It will still be hearty without the marrow).

- When the marrow has cooled to the consistency of softened butter (like what you would use for making cookies), place it in the bowl of a mixer fitted with a whisk attachment. Whip it until it is white and fluffy, like whipped butter. Whip in herbs and season with salt and pepper to taste. You can cook with this whipped marrow like you would cook with butter, or you can spread it on toast with a squeeze of lemon.

94. Roman Style Oxtail Ragu

Serving: Serves 6 | Prep: | Cook: | Ready in:

Ingredients

- 1500 grams Oxtail pieces
- olive oil
- salt
- freshly ground black pepper
- 1 celery stick, peeled and diced
- 1 small carrot, peeled and diced
- 1 onion, peeled and diced
- 3 garlic cloves, peeled and finely sliced
- 250 milliliters red wine
- 125 milliliters beef stock
- 1 bottle (roughly 700g) passata
- 400 grams tinned crushed tomatoes
- 1 tablespoon dried oregano

Direction

- Splash a good lug of olive oil into a heavy based pot and place on medium-high heat. Add the oxtail, in batches, and season with a little salt and pepper. Cook, turning every now and then until brown and caramelised. Remove from the pot and set aside.
- Add the celery, carrot and onion to the pot with a little more olive oil. Lower the heat to medium and cook, stirring, until soft and translucent. Add the garlic and cook for another 2 minutes.
- Return the browned oxtail to the pot, turn the heat up to high and add the wine. Give everything a good stir, dislodging any brown bits that have caught on the bottom of the pot. Let the wine bubble away for 2 – 3 minutes, or until reduced by half, then add the beef stock. Simmer for 2 minutes
- Pour in the passata, crushed tomatoes and 200ml water (or just half fill the tin from the tomatoes, swirl around and tip into the pot). Add the oregano, a little more salt and pepper and stir to combine. The oxtail should be almost totally covered. If not, add a little more water.
- Bring to the boil, then turn the heat down to very low, cover, and simmer away for at least 4 hours. You will know it is ready when the oxtail is fork-tender and almost falling from the bone and the oily surface of the sauce is a rich rust colour. Make sure to give everything a good stir every hour or so to avoid the meat catching. Once tender, take the lid off, and remove the oxtail. Increase the heat to medium and allow the sauce to gently simmer and thicken. Spoon off some of the fat that has risen to the surface.
- Meanwhile, shred the meat from the bones, discarding any fatty, gristly bits, and return to the sauce. Stir and taste. Add more salt and pepper if necessary.
- Serve this ragu tossed through fettuccine. Offer chili flakes and parmesan cheese for those who want it, but I think it's perfect just as it is. Make sure there is bread on the table to wipe up any sauce left on the bottom of the plate

95. Rosemary Roasted Turkey

Serving: Serves 2 | Prep: 0hours10mins | Cook: 0hours20mins |Ready in:

Ingredients

- ¾ cup olive oil
- 3 tablespoons minced garlic
- 2 tablespoons chopped fresh rosemary
- 1 tablespoon chopped fresh basil
- 1 tablespoon Italian seasoning
- 1 teaspoon ground black pepper
- salt to taste
- 1 (12 pound) whole turkey

Direction

- Preheat oven to 325 degrees F (165 degrees C).
- In a small bowl, mix the olive oil, garlic, rosemary, basil, Italian seasoning, black pepper and salt. Set aside.
- Wash the turkey inside and out; pat dry. Remove any large fat deposits. Loosen the skin from the breast. This is done by slowly working your fingers between the breast and the skin. Work it loose to the end of the drumstick, being careful not to tear the skin.
- Using your hand, spread a generous amount of the rosemary mixture under the breast skin and down the thigh and leg. Rub the remainder of the rosemary mixture over the outside of the breast. Use toothpicks to seal skin over any exposed breast meat.
- Place the turkey on a rack in a roasting pan. Add about 1/4 inch of water to the bottom of the pan. Roast in the preheated oven 3 to 4 hours, or until the internal temperature of the bird reaches 180 degrees F (80 degrees C).
- Nutrition Facts
- Per Serving:
- 597 calories; protein 68.1g 136% DV; carbohydrates 0.8g; fat 33.7g 52% DV; cholesterol 198.3mg 66% DV; sodium 165.1mg 7% DV.

96. Salt And Pepper Kugel

Serving: Serves at least 15 | Prep: | Cook: |Ready in:

Ingredients

- 0.5 cups schmaltz (details below on how to render your own)
- 1 pound fine noodles
- a few (or more) chicken livers (raw is preferable, though not necessary)
- 1 onion
- 6 eggs, separated
- salt
- pepper

Direction

- Boil, drain, and cool a pound of fine noodles.
- Put the noodles in a 9" x 13" baking dish. Stir in six egg yolks and salt & pepper to taste — be generous!
- Stir a half-cup of schmaltz into the noodle mixture. (To make schmaltz, take a pound of chicken fat, cut into small pieces, and render with an onion in a small frying pan. You're done when the fat is golden-brown and no white fat is left. Pour through a fine mesh sieve to separate the liquid from the solids. Cool before adding to the noodles.)
- Chop the chicken livers into quarters and sauté with a diced onion. When cool, chop into smaller pieces and mix into the noodles.
- Fold in six egg whites, beaten.
- Bake for an hour at 350 degrees. The noodles at the top should be crispy, and the edges of the kugel should be nice and brown. (Don't worry about over baking -- in my family we prefer the edges to be burnt.)

97. Sautéed Frog Legs W/ Chubritza

Serving: Serves 6-8 | Prep: | Cook: |Ready in:

Ingredients

- 1 pound frog legs
- A few tablespoons Chubritza (for dipping)

- flour
- 2 eggs (beaten)
- salt
- pepper
- oregeno
- paprika
- olive oil
- butter

Direction

- Wash and dry frog legs completely
- Dip legs in flour mixed with salt, pepper, oregano and paprika; then dip in egg wash.
- Sauté in olive oil and butter until golden (depending on size of legs – approximately 3 minutes per side).
- Serve while hot. Dip in Chubritza set out in small dipping plates.
- Note: If you don't have or can't find Chubritza, this recipe can also be made just dipped in flour, without the egg wash and eaten plain...yummy little buttery snacks!

98. Slow Cooker Venison Roast

Serving: Makes your financial life a pain in the ass | Prep: 0hours30mins | Cook: 0hours1mins | Ready in:

Ingredients

- 3 pounds boneless venison roast
- 1 large onion, sliced
- 1 tablespoon soy sauce
- 1 tablespoon Worcestershire sauce
- 1 tablespoon garlic salt
- ¼ teaspoon ground black pepper
- 1 (1 ounce) package dry onion soup mix
- 1 (10.75 ounce) can condensed cream of mushroom soup

Direction

- Put cleaned meat in slow cooker and cover with onion. Sprinkle with soy sauce, Worcestershire sauce, garlic salt and pepper.
- In a small bowl combine the soup mix and the soup; mix together and pour mixture over venison. Cook on Low setting for 6 hours.
- Nutrition Facts
- Per Serving:
- 314 calories; protein 48g 96% DV; carbohydrates 10g 3% DV; fat 8g 12% DV; cholesterol 171.3mg 57% DV; sodium 1881.7mg 75% DV.

99. Spare The Angst Classic Turkey Gravy

Serving: Serves 8 to 12 | Prep: | Cook: | Ready in:

Ingredients

- 1 turkey neck and wing tips
- 1/2 onion, sliced
- 1 carrot, thickly sliced
- 1 stalk celery, thickly sliced
- 1 bay leaf
- Salt and pepper
- 4 to 5 tablespoons flour
- Low salt chicken broth, as needed

Direction

- As soon as the turkey goes in the oven, put the turkey neck and the wing tips (if you have cut them off the turkey) in a large saucepan with the onion, carrot, celery and bay leaf. Add a pinch of salt and a few grindings of black pepper. Cover with about an inch of water and bring to a boil over medium heat. Decrease the heat so that the stock simmers gently while the turkey roasts, for at least one hour. Just be sure the liquid doesn't boil away (add more if necessary). Strain the stock.
- When the turkey is done, remove it from the roasting pan and set it on a platter to rest for a while before carving (at least 30 minutes.)

- Pour all the drippings--the juices and fat-- from the roasting pan into a large (4 cup) Pyrex measuring cup or glass bowl. Let it rest for about 5 minutes to allow the fat to separate and rise to the top. Skim off and discard the fat.
- Pour about 1 cup of the turkey stock you made in step one into the roasting pan and stir with a whisk to release all the brown bits from the bottom of the pan. Add the turkey drippings (now de-fatted) to the pan and stir some more. Strain all of this back into the measuring cup to see how much you have and to rid the stock of any unwanted crusty bits from the bottom of the pan. Add enough turkey stock to the measuring cup to make four cups. If you don't have enough stock, add chicken broth. Pour it into a saucepan.
- Mix the flour with 1/3 cup cold water until smooth, using a gravy shaker, or whisking it in a bowl to smooth out the lumps. Strain if you can't get the lumps out. Whisk this slurry into the stock and bring it to a boil. Simmer for at least 5 minutes to rid the gravy of the raw flour taste. The amount of flour depends on your taste. My view on this is that it should be fairly thin; the flour should just add a little body to the stock without making it goopy. If you want thicker gravy, repeat the flour and water exercise, and add it cautiously and in increments to the gravy. It will thicken as it cooks, so give it a little time (5 to 6 minutes) before you jump in with more flour. Season with salt and pepper.

100. Spicy Plum Glazed Duck And Nectarine Salad

Serving: Makes 2 servings | Prep: | Cook: |Ready in:

Ingredients

- For the spicy plum glaze
- 2 purple plums, pitted and diced
- 1 garlic clove grated on a microplane or put through a garlic press
- 1 teaspoon grated fresh ginger
- 4 tablespoons honey, divided (2/2)
- 3 tablespoons soy sauce
- 3 tablespoons rice vinegar
- 1 tablespoon granulated sugar
- 1 tablespoon sambal oelek
- For the salad and duck
- two 7 to 8 ounce duck breasts, skin on
- one head of romaine lettuce, shredded
- 2 nectarines, pitted and sliced into wedges
- Extra Virgin olive oil and salt
- The spicy plum glaze

Direction

- For the spicy plum glaze
- In a small sauce pan, combine all ingredients but only two tablespoons of the honey. Bring up to a simmer and simmer for about 10 to 12 minutes.
- Off the heat, blend the mixture with an immersion blender until relatively smooth. Whisk in the remaining 2 tablespoons of honey.
- For the salad and duck
- Score the skin of the duck breasts in a cross hatch pattern. Lightly salt the skin side and then place skin side down in a large oven proof skillet. Place over medium low heat and cook the breasts for 8 to 12 minutes until the skin is crispy, lightly browned and much of the fat has rendered.
- Pre heat your oven to 350F. Flip the breasts and lightly brush a little of the glaze over the skin side. Place in the oven and roast for about 10 minutes or until the breasts reach an internal temp of about 155F. Remove from the pan and let the breasts rest for a few minutes while you make the salad.
- Warm the glaze and then toss the shredded lettuce with a tablespoon or two of extra virgin olive oil and a little salt.
- Divide the lettuce on to two dinner plates and decoratively place the nectarine wedges around.

- Slice the duck breasts and place the slices over the lettuce and nectarines. Drizzle as much of the glaze as you like over.

101. Spicy Venison Chili

Serving: Serves 8 -10 | Prep: 0hours30mins | Cook: 5hours0mins | Ready in:

Ingredients

- 2 tablespoons Olive Oil
- 1 Yellow Onion, Diced
- 3 Large Cloves of Garlic, minced
- 5 Jalapeno Peppers, 3 roughly chopped, 2 minced
- 2 pounds Venison (or beef substitute)
- 2 14 oz. cans of fire roasted tomatoes
- 1 can of Tomato sauce
- 1 cup Venison Stock (or beef substitute)
- 1 tablespoon Red Chili Powder
- 2 tablespoons Ancho Chli Powder
- 3 tablespoons Oregano
- 1 tablespoon Sea Salt (or to taste)
- 1 teaspoon Cayenne Pepper
- 2 teaspoons Red Pepper Flakes
- 2 teaspoons Cumin
- 1 bunch Cilantro, for garnish

Direction

- Prepare the meat: If using venison, be sure to get all the silver skin off the meat. Slice into thick 2" chunks.
- In a Dutch oven, warm olive oil at med. high heat. Add onions and cook until it begins to 'sweat".
- Add garlic and peppers and slowly cook for a few more minutes until tender.
- Next add Venison/Beef and begin to brown the meat (if using venison, work fast as it is very lean and be easily overcooked).
- Remove from heat and transfer mixture to a Slow Cooker/Crock Pot. Add all remaining ingredients and mix thoroughly. Cover and cook on low for 4-6 hours or more until meat is tender, stirring periodically. Depending on your slow cooker, low can sometimes be too hot. If you notice after several hours your sauce is bubbling or burning around edges, turn heat down to warm. It should barely be at a constant simmer. The longer and lower the heat, the more tender your meat will be!
- Garnish with cilantro. Serve with Sweet Cornbread or on top of a baked potato.

102. Spicy Chipotle Bison Burger

Serving: Makes 4 1/2 lb burger patties | Prep: | Cook: | Ready in:

Ingredients

- Bison burger patty
- 2 pounds Ground Bison meat
- 2 tablespoons Worcestershire sauce
- 2 teaspoons Good quality sea salt
- 8 Slices of sharp cheddar
- Bunch Of baby salad greens
- 1 Small Vidalia onion
- 1 Small organic tomato
- 4 Pretzel buns
- Chipotle mayonnaise
- 6 ounces Mayonnaise
- 1 Small can of chipotle peppers in adobo
- Splash Worcestershire sauce

Direction

- Add salt, pepper and shire sauce to ground bison and mix by hand. Form the bison into 4 1/2 burger patties. Heat a medium skillet and add a Glug of olive oil. Place patties in pan and cook each side for about 6 minutes. Add a splash of water the pan and put lid on until burgers reach a temp of 135. Remove lid and place 2 slices of cheese on each patty. Put lid back on until the cheese covers the sides of the burger and the internal temp reaches 140-145

degrees for a medium burger. Place burgers on a plate to rest. Meanwhile prepare chipotle mayo.
- Put mayo, shire sauce and chipotle peppers in a food processor until smooth. Build your burger! Smear a healthy amount of mayo on the bottom of your bun, top with onion slices, tomato slices, baby greens and finally the burger and bun top. Hold with two hands and use lots of napkins.

103. Sweet And Sour Roast Goose With Autumn Squash And Cranberries

Serving: Serves 6 to 8 | Prep: | Cook: | Ready in:

Ingredients

- 1 whole goose, about 10 pounds
- Coarse salt
- 1 pinch crushed juniper
- 1 large butternut squash (peeled, seeded, and cut into 2 inch chunks
- 1 cup cranberries
- 1/4 cup maple syrup
- 2 tablespoons maple vinegar
- 1 teaspoon coarse mustard

Direction

- Rinse and dry the goose with paper towels. Rub it inside and out with the salt and refrigerate, uncovered, for at least 6 hours or overnight. Then pat it dry with paper towels, set it on a rack, and allow it to come to room temperature, about an hour. Trim any excess fat from the goose and reserve for another use. Using the tip of a sharp knife, lightly score the breast and leg skin in a crosshatch pattern. This helps to render the fat more quickly during roasting.
- Preheat the oven to 325°F. Season the goose with a little more salt and the ground juniper. Place the goose on a rack in a deep roasting pan and roast for about an hour. Every 30 minutes or so, baste the bird with the pan juices; then pour off the fat through a sieve into a large heatproof bowl (and reserve it for later use). Reduce the heat to 275°F, add the cubed squash and cranberries to the pan, and return the goose to the oven. Continue roasting until a thermometer registers 165°F at the center of the breast, about 1½ to 2 hours. Total roasting time is about 3 hours.
- In a small dish, whisk together the maple syrup, vinegar, and mustard to make a glaze. Brush the goose with the glaze several minutes before removing it from the oven. When it is done, place the goose on a carving board and allow to rest for 20 to 30 minutes before carving. Serve the goose with the squash and cranberries drizzled with the pan juices.

104. Tea Smoked Whole Duck With Plum Wine Sauce

Serving: Serves 2-4 | Prep: | Cook: | Ready in:

Ingredients

- Day 1, 24-hour marinade
- one 5-pound whole duck
- 1 cup water
- 1 cup low salt soy sauce
- 1/2 cup honey
- 1/2 cup maple syrup
- 4 cloves garlic, chopped
- one 3-inch piece ginger, peeled and chopped
- 1 whole lemon, halved
- 1 whole lime, halved
- 2 tangerines, halved
- Day 2, Smoking the Duck
- 1/2 cup black tea (mango black, lapsang souchang, etc)
- 1 cup white rice (use a cheap white rice as you'll be tossing it later)
- 1/4 cup white sugar
- Plum Wine Sauce:

- 1 cup plum wine
- 1/4 cup rice wine vinegar
- 1/2 cup water
- 1 tablespoon soy sauce
- Juice of 2 tangerines
- 1 teaspoon cornstarch
- one 1-inch piece ginger, peeled and sliced into thin strips
- 1 large garlic clove, chopped roughly
- 1 teaspoon kosher salt

Direction

- Day 1, 24 Hour Marinade: In a large bowl, mix the water, soy sauce, honey, maple syrup, garlic, ginger and the juice of the lemon, lime and tangerines (save the spent citrus). Remove the giblets, liver, and any other treats from inside the cavity and pierce the skin of the duck all over with a fork (especially satisfying after a long day at the office). Fill the duck's cavity with the spent citrus. Place the marinade liquid and duck inside and extra-large plastic bag and then seal the bag. I like to place the bag into a large bowl in case the bag breaks or moving things around in the fridge pierces the bag accidentally. Marinate the duck for at least 24 hours.
- Day 2, Smoking the Flavors: Line the bottom of your wok with aluminum foil and layer long sheets of aluminum (high enough to cover the duck completely) every few inches so there are no gaps in the foil. You're basically creating a tent for the duck. Place the steamer insert inside the wok and turn the heat to high. Heat the rice until it starts to smoke. Before placing the duck, breast side up, on top of the steam insert, pat it dry and cover it completely so no steam can escape.
- On medium low heat, steam the duck for 20 minutes. Turn the stove off and, keeping it covered, let it rest under the aluminum tent for an additional 10 minutes. Preheat your oven to 375°. Place the duck (throw the rice and tea away) into a roasting pan and roast the duck for 1 hour and 15 minutes, or until the skin starts turning crispy. If you're going to reserve the drained fat for use in other recipes, do this while the fat is still in its liquid state. Let the duck rest for a few minutes before cutting into the meat.
- Plum Wine Sauce: For the last 30 minutes of roasting, put all of the sauce ingredients into a pan and cook for 20 minutes or until the sauce has reduced and becomes thick. Remove the peels and garlic and reserve the sauce as a glaze over the duck.

105. Thanksgiving Turkey, Dressing, And Cranberry Monte Cristo

Serving: Serves 4 | Prep: | Cook: | Ready in:

Ingredients

- 8 slices sandwich bread (white, wheat, whatever)
- Leftover turkey meat, sliced to uniform thickness
- Mayonnaise
- Leftover stuffing/dressing
- Leftover cranberry sauce
- 2 large eggs
- 1/4 cup half and half
- salt
- ground black pepper
- 4 tablespoons butter

Direction

- Lightly spread mayonnaise on one side of each slice of bread. Start layering turkey onto the mayo side of a slice of bread to within ½ inch of edge on all sides. Top the turkey with cranberry sauce. Top the cranberry sauce with dressing (this order keeps the bread from sogging out from the cranberry sauce). Place a second slice of bread onto the dressing (mayo side to dressing).
- Slice the crust off the bread. Press the edges together. Press the sandwich with a flat

surface utensil, plate, skillet, whatever, to compact the bread.
- In a bowl, beat eggs and whisk in ¼ cup half and half. Season with a pinch of salt and pepper.
- Heat half the butter in a skillet over medium heat. When melted, dredge pressed sandwich in the egg wash, making sure all sides are coated. The egg won't completely absorb into the bread as you normally see with French toast because it's been compressed. Cook for 3-4 minutes per side until sandwich is golden brown. Also, upend the sandwich to cook on the ends until golden. Repeat with remaining sandwiches, adding butter to skillet as needed.
- Cut the sandwich diagonally and eat immediately.

106. The Most Requested Pâté Ever

Serving: Serves many | Prep: 0hours20mins | Cook: 1hours0mins | Ready in:

Ingredients

- 2 lbs chicken livers
- 4 strips bacon (applewood smoked if you can get it)
- 1 large sweet onion
- 2 granny smith apples
- 2 sticks unsalted butter
- 6 fresh sage leaves
- 1/2 teaspoon fresh ground nutmeg
- 1/2 cup calvados (or brandy if you can't get your hands on calvados)
- salt and pepper
- minced red onion - GARNISH
- cornichon - GARNISH
- chopped boiled egg - GARNISH
- capers - GARNISH
- dijon mustard - GARNISH

Direction

- Peel and chop the onion. Peel, core and chop the apples. Don't worry about finesse - they will all get ground up later.
- Put the chicken livers in a colander, rinse thoroughly, trim membranes and weird green things, and leave them in the sink to drain (note - these can be used to frighten children until you cook them!)
- Cook the bacon in the largest skillet you own. Cook it until it is quite crisp, and remove it - set aside.
- Add 2 tbs of the butter and onions to the skillet (yes, leave that bacon fat in there) and cook them over medium heat until they are caramelized and a nice golden brown. Now add remaining butter, and the apples and cook the whole lot until the apples are very tender.
- Add the chicken livers and calvados, and cook until the livers are cooked through.
- Turn off the heat, chop and add the sage leaves and nutmeg, taste the liquid and add some fresh ground black pepper. Break the bacon up and add that too.
- Working in batches, put the liver mixture in the food processor and process until fairly smooth - taste as you go and adjust the salt if needed (the bacon adds salt which is why you wait). Put each batch in a large bowl when it is processed so you can mix the whole thing together at the end.
- Put in bowls or tupperware, chill, freeze, or keep warm if you are serving it right away. Serve with any or all of the following (I like to put each garnish in a separate little bowl for serving - it looks nice and gives your guests the choice of which they prefer): minced red onion, chopped boiled egg, capers, cornichon, Dijon mustard

107. Tower Of Duck Gizzards Salad

Serving: Serves 1-6 depending on hungriness of eaters | Prep: | Cook: | Ready in:

Ingredients

- 1 pound duck gizzards
- salt
- pepper
- 1/2 cup all purpose flour
- 1 teaspoon seasoning salt
- 2 teaspoons fresh thyme
- 1-2 bunches frisee salad
- juice from 1/2 lemon
- 2-3 tablespoons olive oil
- 1/4 cup grapeseed oil

Direction

- Wash duck gizzards and boil in salted water for about one hour, until tender.
- Take out of water. Drain and cool.
- Meanwhile, mix flour, seasoning salt, fresh thyme, and fresh ground pepper together in flat dish. And dip and roll gizzards lightly in flour mixture.
- Heat grape seed oil in large skillet and fry gizzards over medium high heat until golden. Remove and drain.
- Wash and dry frisee salad and dress with lemon, olive oil and salt and pepper to taste. Arrange on large platter. Arrange fried duck gizzards on top in towering pyramid shape and indulge.

108. Tripe With Chickpeas And Chorizo

Serving: Serves 6 | Prep: | Cook: | Ready in:

Ingredients

- 250 grams dry chickpeas
- 1000 grams tripe (preferably cleaned and purified)
- 120 milliliters vinegar (optional, in case your tripe isn't cleaned or purified)
- 6   bay leaves
- 6   cloves of garlic
- 2   onions
- 1   carrot
- 2 tablespoons smoked paprika
- 1   good quality chorizo sausage for stewing
- 300 milliliters white wine
- 1 liter good quality chicken stock (homemade if possible)

Direction

- First of all, you have to soak the chickpeas overnight in a covered bowl. Make sure the amount of water is about double as high as the chickpeas as they will double in size. You could use chickpeas out of a can, but you'll never get the same pleasing al dente texture which gives this dish a very necessary bite.
- Next, you have to prepare the tripe. Ask your butcher to make sure that your tripe is cleaned and ready to cook. If you can't get your hands on clean tripe, you'll have to purify it by first removing excess fat from the side opposite the honeycomb which is whiter than the creamy color of the tripe. Then you rub and scrub the tripe thoroughly all over with course sea salt. Rinse several times with water, place in a dish and pour the vinegar over it. Let stand for 30 minutes and then rinse well. Congratulations, now your tripe is ready for cooking!
- From here, it's long but easy sailing: cook your tripe, covered in water with 3 bay leaves and 2 crushed garlic cloves. You can cook it in a pressure cooker for half an hour or simmer it for three hours in a normal pan on medium heat. It should be tender and soft, if it isn't yet, cook it a bit more but make sure it still got a bit of a bite to it so it doesn't fall apart by the time you get to the end of the dish. Always make sure your tripe is continuously covered in water when cooked. When cooked, drain, remove bay leaves and garlic, let cool and cut into strips of 4 cm. It doesn't matter if it's a bit irregularly shaped, this is rural cooking and adds to the charm.
- With regards to the chickpeas: drain and wash them thoroughly. To facilitate digestion, first cook them for 10 minutes, pour out the water

and add new water and cook for another 30 minutes until al dente (be aware that chickpeas you've had laying around in your cupboard will have to cook longer), drain and set aside. Now you're ready to put the recipe together.

- Roughly chop up your onion, peel and chop up your carrot into the same size (it doesn't have to be fine, you want it to be chunky and rustic) and sweat in a big pot on a medium heat in olive oil. Add a bit of salt to help the onion break down and release its sweetness. In the meantime, chop up the garlic quite finely and when the onions are translucent, add your garlic and stir. Let cook for about 4 minutes.
- Meanwhile, rinse the chorizo under cold water, put the tip of your knife under the skin, tear it off and cut into bite-size chunks. Add the chorizo and stir until the chorizo starts to release its deep red color.
- Add paprika powder, the three remaining bay leaves, stir and let fry for another minute or so to allow the paprika to "wake up".
- Next, add your glass of wine and let it simmer for five minutes until your wine has reduced by half. This is when you add your chickpeas, tripe and chicken stock. With the lid off, let the stew simmer on a low heat, stirring every once in a while, and let reduce until the whole dish has transformed from a watery soup to a thick, unctuous stew. This should take about 30 minutes.
- Taste and season with salt and freshly ground black pepper. If you love paprika as much as I do, you probably won't be able to resist adding just a bit more before you serve it in your most beautiful earthenware dish with some crusty bread in the middle of the table and let everyone dig in.

109. Truffled Chicken Mousse

Serving: Serves 20-30 | Prep: | Cook: | Ready in:

Ingredients

- 1.5 pounds Free range chicken livers
- 2 cups Milk
- 3 Sticks unsalted butter (room temperature)
- 1 cup Diced shallots
- 1 tablespoon Dried french tarragon (or twice as much fresh)
- 1 teaspoon White pepper
- 1 teaspoon Freshly ground black pepper
- 1/2 cup Madeira
- 3 teaspoons Kosher salt
- 1/4 cup Light cream
- 3 Farm fresh egg yolks
- 1 black truffle

Direction

- Rinse livers in cold water and soak in milk overnight in the fridge.
- The next day, set the butter out and bring to room temperature. Pour the livers into a colander and let strain. Stir the livers with your hand to loosen any pockets of milk, but do not rinse. Discard the milk
- Melt 3 Tbsp. of butter in a medium pan, add the shallots and sauté on low heat. Do not let them brown. Add the tarragon, white pepper & black pepper. Lightly sauté until the shallots are soft and just starting to stick to the pan. Deglaze with 1/4 cup Madeira and scrape the pan of any bits. Reduce the liquid by 2/3 to 3/4, stirring occasionally. Scrape the mixture into a food processor equipped with the metal blade.
- Return the pan to the flame, add 3 Tbsp. of butter and increase to medium heat. Sauté the chicken livers in small batches, turning over after 2-3 minutes. Do not crowd the livers. The liver should be lightly browned, but still slightly pink on the interior. Transfer each batch to the food processor when cooked. After the last batch of livers is complete, deglaze the pan with the remaining 1/4 cup Madeira and reduce by 2/3. Stir frequently to incorporate any bits of liver and add to the food processor.

- Add the cream and salt to the liver mix. Dice the truffle and add to the mix. Cover the food processor and begin chopping. While mixing, add one stick of butter in 2 Tbsp. chunks, then the egg yolks and remaining butter in 2 Tbsp. chunks and continue processing until the pate is smooth and uniform. It should have the texture of a semi-thick sauce. Only use fresh local eggs for this step, otherwise simply skip them.
- Pour the pate into a medium strainer and push through with a spatula. Transfer to serving dishes, cover and place in the fridge overnight. Serve with your favorite crackers, bread or crostini. This is a fairly large batch of pate and ready to serve dishes can be frozen for later use.

110. Turkey And Sage Biscuit Pot Pie (Gluten And Dairy Free)

Serving: Serves 4-6 | Prep: | Cook: | Ready in:

Ingredients

- Turkey Pot Pie Filling
- 3 Carrots
- 1 cup Frozen Green Peas
- 1 Potato (Medium)
- 1 Organic Turkey Breast
- 2 Celery Stalks
- 3 Crimini Mushrooms
- 2 tablespoons Arrowroot
- 2 cups Water
- 1/2 teaspoon Sage
- 2 tablespoons Soy Free Vegan Mayonnaise
- Salt and Pepper to taste
- Paleo Herb Biscuits
- 2 cups Almond Meal
- 1/2 cup Coconut Flour
- 5 Egg whites
- 5 tablespoons Coconut Oil
- 1/4-1/2 Fresh Herbs (Thyme, Rosemary, Sage)
- 1 tablespoon Apple Cider Vinegar
- 1 pinch Salt

Direction

- Turkey Pot Pie Filling
- Preheat the oven to 425F. Poach the turkey breast (or cutlets) in the 2 cups of water, about 5 minutes. Remove the turkey from the water (do not discard the water) and allow it to cool on a cutting board.
- While the turkey is cooling, dice the carrots, celery, potato and mushrooms.
- Shred the turkey. Add the turkey, chopped vegetables and peas to the rectangular baking dish, mixing as you distribute them in the dish. I used a ceramic baking dish, unlined (6"x10").
- To the poaching liquid, add 2 Tbsp. of arrowroot and 2 Tbsp. of vegan mayo. Heat over a medium flame until it thickens and then add salt, pepper and ground sage. It will be very thick but the vegetables will release a lot of water while they cook, thinning it out considerably.
- Pour the gravy over the vegetable and turkey mixture. Cover with a lid or aluminum foil and bake at 425F for 20-25 minutes.
- Remove the baking dish from the oven and reduce the temperature to 350F.
- Paleo Herb Biscuits
- Mix all of the ingredients in a bowl until it forms a thick paste.
- Take the baking dish out of the oven and remove the aluminum foil.
- With your hands form the dough into 2-3" biscuit rounds and lay them gently across the top of the pot pie mixture.
- Return the dish to the oven and bake at 350F for 10-15 minutes or until the biscuits are golden brown around the edges.

111. Tuscan Chicken Liver Paté

Serving: Makes about 2 dozen crostini | Prep: 0hours15mins | Cook: 0hours15mins | Ready in:

Ingredients

- 1 pound organic chicken livers
- 2 tablespoons extra-virgin olive oil
- 2 tablespoons unsalted butter
- 2 large shallots, thinly sliced
- 1 large clove garlic, smashed
- 3 anchovy filets (or 1 tablespoon anchovy paste)
- 1 tablespoon capers, minced
- 5 sage leaves
- 2/3 cup dry white wine
- 1/2 teaspoon grated lemon zest
- 1/2 cup grated parmigiano reggiano

Direction

- Trim any sinews from the livers and dry well with paper towels.
- In a large skillet, melt the butter and olive oil over medium-high heat. Sauté the shallots, garlic, anchovy, capers and sage until shallots are lightly browned, 6 minutes or so.
- Season the chicken livers with salt and pepper and add to the pan. Cook over high heat until browned, then add half of the white wine (1/3 cup) and keep stirring with a wooden spoon, breaking up the livers as they start to cook through. When the wine is absorbed, add the second 1/3 cup and repeat the process.
- Remove from heat and transfer to a food processor. Process until quite smooth, then add lemon zest and cheese and process again. Taste and add salt or pepper as needed. Serve warm or at room temperature to spread on grilled country bread.

112. Tuscan Inspired Bison Stew

Serving: Serves 4 | Prep: | Cook: | Ready in:

Ingredients

- 1 pound Bison Stew Meat
- 1/4 pound Pancetta
- 3/4 cup Olive Oil
- 3 sprigs Rosemary
- 3 sprigs Thyme
- 3-4 Basil Leaves-Chiffonade
- 4 Garlic Smashed
- 3 Cloves Roasted Garlic
- 1/2 cup Sun Dried Tomatos in Oil
- 2 Cans Diced Tomato
- 4 Anchovies
- 1 tablespoon Capers-Drained
- 1 cup Red Wine- Supertuscan or Chianti
- 1 cup Beef Broth
- Salt and Pepper to Taste

Direction

- Marinate the bison in the olive oil, rosemary, thyme, and 2 cloves of garlic + salt and pepper for 3-4 hours. (Make sure to rub the meat around in the marinade every hour or so.)
- Render the pancetta in a tablespoon of the marinade and remove with a slotted spoon and set aside. Add two smashed garlic cloves and once they start singing and become aromatic remove them and set aside. Add the anchovies and smash with the back of a spoon until they have become incorporated in the oil.
- Sear the bison meat on all sides and remove from pot. Add the sundried tomatoes, canned tomatoes, roasted garlic, wine and capers, stirring the bits off the bottom of the pan, turn the heat up to medium-high and let the mixture reduce by half.
- Add the bison back to the pot, along with the beef broth and the rosemary, thyme, basil, salt and pepper. Turn the heat to low, cover and simmer for two hours. Remove the lid and continue to simmer until it reaches your

desired consistency. This can be a very thick ragu, or a more loose stew.
- Serve over rigatoni or with risotto and add some shaved parmesan and fresh Italian parsley.

- Note 2: In Tuscany, the traditional pâté made in the countryside is chopped by hand with a knife so it's more granulated. I blend it to get a smoother paste because I like it better this way. If you want a softer and smoother paste, add 1 tablespoon of soft butter when processing the pâté and blend more time.

113. Tuscan Liver Crostini Crostini Di Fegatini Toscani

Serving: Serves 6 | Prep: | Cook: | Ready in:

Ingredients

- 6 very fresh chicken livers chopped roughly
- 2 very fresh chicken hearts chopped roughly
- 1/2 red onion chopped finely
- 2 fresh sage leaves
- 4 tablespoons Extra Virgin Olive Oil
- 1 tablespoon salted capers
- 5 tablespoons Vin Santo
- Salt
- Pepper

Direction

- Clean, trim and devein the chicken livers and hearts and chop roughly.
- Wash the salted capers with cold water and then leave them 15 minutes in a bowl with cold water. Pat dry and set aside.
- Chop the onion finely.
- In a pan, add the olive oil, onion and sage leafs. When the onion is translucent add the chicken livers and hearts, stir and allow to brown on all sides, about 4 minutes. Add the capers and the Vin Santo and stir to mix well. Simmer on low temperature about 10 minutes.
- Remove from the heat, discard the sage leaves and process with an immersion hand blender.
- Season with salt and pepper.
- Cut Italian bread in slices, lightly toast them and spread the liver pâté on the toasts and serve immediately.
- Note 1: the liver pâté can be made well in advance. Toast the bread when serving it.

114. Vanilla Spiced Duck Confit

Serving: Serves 4 | Prep: | Cook: | Ready in:

Ingredients

- Whole Duck, quartered, Cooking Of Duck Confit
- 1 Whole Duck, quartered
- 3 pieces Star Anise
- 2 bunches Fresh Thyme
- 1 Cinnamon Stick
- 2 Vanilla Beans, split
- 2 Cloves, garlic crushed
- .25 cups Juniper Berries
- 1 cup Kosher Salt
- 1 cup Brown Sugar, light
- 4 cups Grape-seed Oil
- Israeli Couscous with Red Currents
- 1 pound Tri Colored Israeli Couscous
- 3 quarts Water, tap cold
- 3 tablespoons Kosher Salt
- 2 tablespoons Olive Oil
- 1 cup Dried Red Currents
- 1 bunch Fresh Mint, picked and chopped, no stems

Direction

- Purchase a whole duck from your local butcher, preferably butchered into quartos for you.
- Measure out salt and sugar, mix together and generously rub all aspects of the quartered duck, place the duck into a large container and

- allow to rest in the refrigerator for approx. 2 days.
- Once the duck has marinated, rinse the excess salt and sugar mixture off, before placing into a large Dutch oven or casserole dish.
- In a large bowl add star anise, cinnamon sticks, split vanilla bean, crushed garlic, juniper berries, mix until all ingredients are incorporated.
- Place the pour the oil over the quartered duck until it is just covered all aspects of the duck.
- Preheat the oven to 200F, cover the Dutch oven or large casserole with either the lid or aluminum foil.
- Bake for 5-6 hours, the duck should be fork tender, if not continue to cook.
- Once the duck has cooked remove from the oven carefully, place the dish onto a hot plate and reserve for platting.
- For the couscous, add water to a medium size sauce pot, followed by the salt, and olive oil.
- Bring the water to a boil, carefully add the couscous, and cook for approx. 12 minutes until soft.
- Strain the couscous through a colander of strainer, add the dried currents and chopped mint to the couscous.
- For platting, remove the duck from the oil, placing onto a large serving platter, on a separate platter, pour the drained couscous and serve.
- Keep the FAT! The confit will keep, refrigerated, for up to 6 months. (When ladling the hot fat, be careful not to disturb any of the juices at the bottom of the pan. You do not want any of these juices to go into the storage containers. Strain the remaining fat through cheesecloth, leaving behind the juices. Pour the juices into a bowl and refrigerate the strained fat and juices separately. The fat can be reused several times until it becomes too salty. The confit juices will set into a jelly.)Label and date.

115. Venison Jerky

Serving: Makes .5 pounds | Prep: | Cook: |Ready in:

Ingredients

- 1 pound venison or lean beef
- 1/4 cup Bragg's Amino Acids
- 1/4 cup Mirin
- 1 tablespoon fresh ground black pepper
- 1 tablespoon garam masala
- 1 tablespoon coarse sea salt
- 1 tablespoon garlic powder

Direction

- Freeze the venison for an hour or so. Cut across the grain into strips about 1/4 inch thick.
- Combine all remaining ingredients in a quart-sized ziploc bag. Blend well. Add strips of venison. Seal and place in refrigerator for 24 hours or so.
- Drain venison and pat dry. Place strips a few inches apart on cloth towels or paper towels and cover with plastic wrap. Pound with a wooden rolling pin to even thickness.
- Set dehydrator or oven to 155 degrees. Place venison strips individually on racks, not touching.
- Dehydrate venison for 24 hours. Allow to cool completely. Store at room temperature in sealed container.

116. Venison Steak And Eggs With Brown Butter Ramps

Serving: Serves 2 | Prep: | Cook: |Ready in:

Ingredients

- 2 Thick cut Venison Steaks
- 2-5 tablespoons Vegetable Oil
- 1/2 (ish) cups Butter
- 4 (ish) tablespoons Salt

- dash Pepper
- 3-5 sprigs Thyme
- half bulb Garlic
- handful Ramps
- 4 Eggs

Direction

- For the Venison Steak: Marinate in an ample amount of salt, vegetable oil, pepper, and garlic. Heat pan to a high temperature with vegetable oil and sear steak until medium rare. Towards the end of cooking add a dollop of butter per steak and a few springs of thyme. Remove from pan and let the steak continue to cook for another 10ish minutes.
- For the ramps: Brown butter. Braise the ramps gently in brown butter with a bit of salt and pepper until tender. Be careful not to overcook.
- For the eggs: How you cook them is up to you but I would suggest either frying them over easy or basting them.

117. Venison And Haggis En Croute

Serving: Serves 4 | Prep: | Cook: |Ready in:

Ingredients

- 300 grams Haggis
- 35 milliliters Whisky
- 450 grams Venison fillet (preferably wild red deer)
- 350 grams Puff pastry
- 1 Egg whisked for eggwash

Direction

- Set the oven to 200C/390F. Mix the haggis with the whisky until is easy to spread.
- Roll the pastry out so that is about 2.5 times the width of the venison and slightly longer at both ends. Place the haggis on the pastry and speed evenly.
- Place the venison in the middle of the pastry and fold over the two sides to meet. Use a little of the eggs 'glue' then fold over the ends and do the same. Place with the joined side down on a pre-greased baking tray and place in the oven for 30-35 minutes until golden brown.
- Remove the cooked venison from the oven, cover in foil and leave to rest for 10 minutes to let the juices soak back into the meat. It should remain moist protected by the fat from the haggis. Serve with mashed potatoes and turnip

118. Vietnamese Style Spicy Pig Ear Salad

Serving: Serves 6 | Prep: | Cook: |Ready in:

Ingredients

- Braising Ingredients
- 1 pound pigs' ears (about 4)
- 1 4-inch knob of ginger, sliced
- 1 stalk of lemongrass, cut into 1" segments and smashed slightly
- 1 small onion, cut into wedges
- 3-5 star anise pods
- 3 cinnamon sticks
- 1/4 cup white vinegar
- 1/2 cup soy sauce
- Salad Ingredients
- 2 bundles mung bean (glass) noodles (or 4 ounces thin rice noodles)
- 2-4 Thai red chili peppers (to taste)
- 1 2-inch segment of lemongrass (use white part of stalk), chopped
- 3 garlic cloves
- 2 limes, juiced
- 1 tablespoon granulated sugar
- 1 tablespoon fish sauce
- 1 tablespoon soy sauce
- 1 cup fresh mint leaves

- 1 cup fresh cilantro leaves and some stems
- 1 cup fresh Thai basil leaves
- 2 cups Vietnamese greens (see note) or watercress
- 1/4 cup roasted peanuts, chopped

Direction

- Remove hair from ears either by shaving them with a razor (nothing makes you feel closer to your food than shaving it!) or by singeing it off over a gas range flame (hold the ears with tongs).
- Bring 3 quarts of water to a boil in a large pot. Add all of the braising ingredients. Slice ears thinly (this may be easier after the ears have been in the boiling broth for about 15 minutes). Reduce heat to low, cover and simmer for 1-2 hours, until tender.
- Shortly before the ears are done, prepare the noodles by boiling them for 2 minutes, or until just soft. Drain and set aside.
- Next, prepare the dressing. In a mortar, grind up chili peppers, lemongrass and garlic to a rough paste. In a bowl, whisk together lime juice, sugar, fish sauce and soy sauce until sugar is dissolved, then add chili paste.
- When the ears are tender remove them from the broth (drain and reserve liquid for another use). Toss together with prepared carrots and greens, noodles and dressing. Top with peanuts and serve immediately.
- Note: If you have access to a good Asian grocery with Vietnamese greens, get a variety of interesting looking ones and mix them together for a nice variety of colors, flavors and textures.

119. Yoghurt Marinated Goat Steaks

Serving: Serves 2 | Prep: | Cook: | Ready in:

Ingredients

- 2 goat steaks, about 1 inch thick each
- 1 cup sheep's milk yoghurt
- 4 medium gloves garlic, minced
- 2 packed tablespoons fresh oregano, chopped
- plenty of sea salt and freshly cracked pepper

Direction

- Season the goat with salt and pepper, being sure to rub it in very well.
- Combine the yoghurt, garlic, and oregano and add this to the goat, again, rubbing it in very well. Allow it to sit overnight.
- Heat your cast iron skillet to medium-high heat and add a small amount of vegetable oil. Cook the steaks quickly – about 2 minutes per side. Goat can dry out very quickly (as I have learned) so watch it closely and don't hesitate to take it off the heat if you think it is drying too much. You are probably right.
- Remove from heat and tent with foil for a few minutes before serving.
- Lastly, if anyone has experience with cooking goat I would love to hear from you. Please feel free to leave suggestions in the comments. Thank you.

120. Braised Rabbit Pappardelle With Mixed Spring Vegetables

Serving: Serves approx. 4 | Prep: | Cook: | Ready in:

Ingredients

- braised rabbit
- 3 ounces pancetta, thickly sliced, or prosciutto ends chopped thinly
- 4 plump garlic cloves, peeled
- 2 to 3 celery ribs and leaves
- 2 tablespoons loosely packed fresh sage leaves, (6 to 8 large leaves)
- 1 small bunch of fresh flat leaf parsley
- 6 or so tablespoons extra-virgin olive oil

- two whole rabbits (fresh or previously frozen & thawed completely), about 3 lbs. or so, cut into serving pieces
- 1 teaspoon sea salt
- 2 tablespoons all-purpose unbleached flour
- ½ to 3/4 cups white wine
- 1 tbsp or so   red-wine vinegar
- 1/2 to 3/4 cups veal broth (or a combination of veal and vegetable broth) homemade preferred
- resh pappardelle egg pasta and spring vegetable mixture
- 3 to 4 large sweet carrots, peeled and cut into small slices
- 1/2 cup or so of fresh baby brussel sprouts (trimmed and sliced in half)
- 1/2 to 3/4 cups fresh frozen baby sweet peas (thawed and drained)
- 1 box   baby frozen artichokes (thawed and drained)
- 2   garlic cloves, peeled and chopped
- sea salt and black pepper
- olive oil
- vegetable stock (homemade preferred)
- homemade fresh cut pappardelle egg noodles (see recipe link) for the pappardelle, roll the pasta dough into thin sheets and then cut the wide strips by hand and lay out to dry.

Direction

- With a food processor, mince the pancetta or prosciutto, garlic, sage, parsley and approximately 2 tablespoons of the olive oil into a fine-textured pestata (like a pesto.)Place the rabbit pieces in a large deep bowl, season all over with the sea salt and black pepper to taste, then sprinkle the flour over all the pieces and toss to coat evenly.
- Pour the remaining olive oil into a deep stock pot and set it over medium-high heat and begin to sauté the pestata. Cook and stir until the pestata has dried a bit and just begins to stick to the bottom of the pan, about 3 to 4 minutes.
- Lay the legs or pieces in the pan in one layer, reduce the heat, and cover the pan. Cook gently for about 10 minutes, allowing the meat to give up its juices and brown very slowly, until all the pieces are lightly golden colored on one side.
- Flip them over, cover the stock pot and slowly brown the second side, about another 10 minutes or so. (If the pot is not large enough for all the pieces, work in batches, remove the first batch and repeat with the second until done).
- Add all the cooked pieces back into the stockpot, add in the celery ribs and leaves and the white wine; sauté this slowly until the wine reduces a bit. Now add the veal or veal & vegetable combo stock and the red wine vinegar to the mixture using a wooden spoon coat the pieces with the stock evenly and adjust the heat until it is cooking at a slow, simmering bubble.
- Leave this to cook, for about 30 minutes or more until the pan juices turn to a thick brown glaze, always turning and tumbling the rabbit pieces as it cooks to ensure even flavor and balance (remove from the heat and set aside to cool.) Once cooled a bit, remove the cooked meat from all the bones, careful as rabbit does have very small bones, etc. Place the rabbit meat back into the stock pot with the pan juices, etc. and set aside for adding to the dish later.
- NOTE: If the pan juices are too thin or watery at the finish, before adding in the de-boned rabbit meat; place the stock pot with the pan juices on medium heat and simmer to reduce for an additional 10 to 15 minutes or so, stir and check this often as it can stick and burn and ruin the final sauce (this final sauce will be used for the pasta dish.)
- In a large deep skillet, drizzle some olive oil and add a few pieces of the chopped garlic, sauté lightly until aromatic. Remove the garlic and discard. Add in the cut carrots and sauté for a moment or two until beginning to brown lightly; add a dose of the stock and stir gently and continue to cook on medium heat until the carrots soften a bit and the liquid reduces.

Remove the carrots from the skillet and reserve the stock in a small bowl.

- Repeat this process with the olive oil and garlic pieces for the baby Brussels sprouts and remove when tender and then repeat the process for the baby artichokes; use the reserved stock from the carrots and add more for each vegetable you are sautéing. Set all the cooked vegetables aside in their separate bowls.
- In a large stock pot of boiling well salted water, cook the pappardelle noodles until soft (they cook very quickly as they are freshly made.) Drain out the noodles and place in a large flat platter and drizzle lightly with olive oil so they do not stick.
- In a large medium deep skillet add your desired amount of the rabbit meat and braised meat sauce from the stock pot. Place on medium low heat until it starts to simmer lightly, add in your cooked Brussels, carrots and artichokes blend gently into the sauce and let simmer very slowly and lightly.
- Add in the fresh peas and chopped tomatoes at the very end, these only need to warm up in the dish for 1 to 2 minutes and they are ready. Now add the cooked pappardelle to the slowly simmering sauce and add more sauce (or a good splash of additional veal stock if the sauce is too thick.) let this simmer slowly, stirring gently until the noodles are well coated. Remove from the heat and season with additional sea salt and pepper to taste before serving; serve immediately with some fresh chopped parsley for flavor and garnish.
- NOTE: Store the remaining rabbit meat in the refrigerator or freezer to add to risotto or future pasta dishes. Reserve and freeze any remaining braising sauce for future dishes as well in a separate container.

121. Cake

Serving: Serves 28 | Prep: 10017hours2mins | Cook: 12345hours23mins | Ready in:

Ingredients

- 234 ounces ketchup
- 2589 bunches mustard
- 3703 liters peanut butter
- 3456 pieces pickle
- 23456 gallons apple
- 234 handfuls anything
- 63 quarts pork

Direction

- Put ketchup in the bowl
- Put everything in any order you'd like then eat right away

122. Duck Magrets With Red Wine Cherries

Serving: Serves 2-4 | Prep: | Cook: | Ready in:

Ingredients

- 500 grams dark cherries, pitted (regular cherries are good, too)
- 3-4 tablespoons honey (like sunflower, acacia)
- 200 milliliters red wine
- 1 sprig rosemary
- 1 good dash of fleshly ground black pepper
- 2 large magrets de canard/duck breast, 400 g eachs

Direction

- In a saucepan, bring red wine and cherries to boil over medium heat.
- Stir in the honey, add the rosemary sprig and season with black pepper.
- Allow to simmer for 5-10 minutes. Serve warm or cold.

- Using your sharpest knife, incise the skin of the magrets in a crosswise pattern (about 1 inch wide).
- In a cast iron pan, place the meat skin side down and fry over medium heat until all fat has rendered (it's ok to place the meat in the cold pan). Spoon out the fat from time to time and save for another time.
- After 15-18 minutes, flip the breast over and fry for another 1-2 minutes. Leave to rest on a plate. Serve with the cherries and potatoes fried in duck fat.

123. Lapin À La Moutarde

Serving: Serves 4-6 | Prep: 0hours20mins | Cook: 1hours0mins | Ready in:

Ingredients

- 1 2-3 pound (if wild) or 3-4 pound (if farmed) rabbit (800 g - 1.2 kg or 1.5 - 2 kg)
- 1/4 cup butter (60g or half a stick)
- 3 shallots, minced
- 4 cloves garlic, minced
- 1 cup white wine or vermouth (250 mL)
- 1/2 cup rabbit or chicken broth (125 mL)
- 1/2 cup heavy cream (125 mL)
- 1/4 cup smooth dijon mustard (60 g)
- 1 tablespoon whole grain dijon mustard (15 g)
- 1 bay leaf
- 1/4 teaspoon powdered sage
- 1/2 teaspoon crushed marjoram leaves
- 1/2 teaspoon crushed oregano leaves
- 1/2 teaspoon crushed savory leaves
- 1/2 teaspoon crushed thyme leaves
- 1/2 teaspoon dried rosemary
- 3-4 pounds small potatoes or potato pieces (1.5")

Direction

- Preheat oven to 350F.
- In a 4 quart (5L) Dutch oven or a similarly sized pot, melt butter on medium heat until just beginning to sizzle.
- Season rabbit parts with salt and pepper. Add to the pot and brown well on all sides. Remove rabbit pieces from pot.
- Add shallots and garlic to hot butter. Stir well and try to scrape up brown bits from the bottom of the pan.
- When shallots and garlic start to brown, add wine or vermouth and stir well.
- Scraping the bottom of the pot the whole time, let mixture boil until slightly thickened and all of the fond is scraped up.
- Add broth first, and then cream. Whisk thoroughly and add mustard and herbs. Lower heat to a simmer.
- Return rabbit pieces to pot and add potatoes. Stir thoroughly to coat all solids with sauce.
- Place pot in the oven uncovered, stirring occasionally, for about an hour. If the liquid is reducing too quickly, cover. Remove from the oven when potatoes are cooked and the rabbit meat is tender.
- Taste before serving and adjust salt as necessary. Add black pepper to taste if desired.

Index

A

Allspice 10
Almond 71
Anchovies 72
Anise 73
Apple 3,6,10,71
Arrowroot 71
Avocado 34

B

Bacon 3,10,26
Basil 3,8,9,72
Beans 5,73
Beef 5,52,65,72
Biscuits 71
Bread 48,52
Broth 3,4,40,45,52,72
Brussels sprouts 78
Buckwheat 3,6
Buns 34
Burger 3,4,10,11,12,39,65
Butter 3,4,5,6,30,52,74

C

Cabbage 10
Cake 3,4,6,78
Capers 72
Carrot 3,4,12,14,15,43,71
Celeriac 3,32
Celery 71
Cheddar 24

Cheese 3,4,12,14,51
Chestnut 3,35
Chicken 3,4,6,7,11,14,15,16,17,18,19,22,29,52,55,57,58,59,70,72
Chickpea 4,69
Chilli 7
Chipotle 3,4,26,65
Chorizo 4,69
Ciabatta 34
Cider 71
Cinnamon 73
Cloves 7,36,65,72,73
Coconut 71
Cognac 31,55
Coriander 3,20
Couscous 73
Cranberry 4,67
Cream 3,4,15,19,54
Crostini 3,4,24,73
Crumble 3,6,12,30
Cucumber 3,8,9,42,43
Cumin 5,65
Curry 3,43

D

Date 3,26
Dijon mustard 55,57,68
Dill 3,19
Duck 3,4,7,10,21,26,27,32,38,44,46,47,51,58,60,64,66,68,73,78

E

Egg 4,45,48,52,71,74,75

F

Fennel 3,27,30
Fig 3,4,30,31,33,51
Flour 48,71

Fruit 4,48

G

Game 1,5,52

Garlic 3,7,12,19,22,34,65,72,75

Ghee 38

Giblets 45

Gin 7

Goose 3,4,34,66

Gorgonzola 10

Gravy 3,4,8,32,49,58,59,63

Grouse 3,39

H

Haggis 4,75

Hare 3,36

Heart 3,4,6,24,60

Herbs 71

Hoisin sauce 16

Honey 3,17,34

Horseradish 4,54

J

Jam 21,52

Jelly 52

Jus 14,40,47,63

K

Kale 3,18,23

L

Lamb 3,4,30,52

Leek 3,18,19

Leftover turkey 67

Lemon 3,7,39

Lime 34

Ling 52

M

Madeira 70

Marrow 4,60

Mayonnaise 65,67,71

Meat 3,12,13,14,15,40,72

Milk 70

Mince 56,60

Mint 73

Mirin 74

Muffins 4,48

Mushroom 52,71

N

Nectarine 4,64

Noodles 3,8,9

Nut 62,63

O

Oil 5,7,10,12,32,34,38,39,65,71,72,73,74

Olive 5,15,21,32,38,39,45,60,65,72,73

Onion 3,5,7,10,12,36,51,65

Oregano 5,65

Oxtail 4,61

P

Paella 3,40

Pancetta 3,33,72

Pappardelle 3,4,24,33,46,76

Parmesan 24

Pastrami 3,28

Pastry 48

Pear 3,27

Peas 71

Pecan 4,45

Peel 14,20,27,32,36,38,68

Pepper 3,4,5,34,39,45,52,60,62,65,71,72,73,75

Pheasant 4,50

Pickle 3,8,9,11

Pie 4,22,46,71

Pistachio 3,30

Pizza 4,51

Plum 3,4,25,64,66,67

Pomegranate 4,52

Porcini 10,52

Port 4,32,52

Potato 3,14,15,22,26,71

Prune 10

Puff pastry 75

Pulse 17,18,24

Q

Quail 3,33

Quark 48

R

Rabbit 3,4,19,29,43,54,55,56,57,76

Raita 3,42,43

Raspberry 3,31,32

Rice 3,15,22,32,38

Risotto 3,25

Rosemary 3,4,33,56,61,71,72

S

Sage 3,4,17,33,45,71

Salad 4,31,64,68,75

Salsa 3,34

Salt 4,5,11,12,21,29,30,32,35,36,39,45,46,52,54,56,60,62,63,65,71,72,73,74

Sausage 3,10,11

Sea salt 33

Seeds 10

Shallot 3,23

Sherry 8

Soup 3,14,15

Squash 4,5,66

Steak 4,74,75,76

Stew 3,4,5,10,36,56,72

Stock 5,7,58,59,65

Stuffing 3,4,35,45

Sugar 34,36,52,73

T

Tea 3,4,22,34,55,66

Terrine 16

Thai basil 9,76

Thyme 3,12,39,71,72,73,75

Tomato 5,10,65,72

Tripe 4,69

Truffle 4,70

Turkey 3,4,8,9,45,49,58,61,63,67,71

V

Vegan 71

Vegetables 4,58,76

Venison 3,4,25,39,45,63,65,74,75

Vinegar 32,52,71

W

Whisky 75

White pepper 70

Wine 4,10,12,36,56,66,67,72,78

Worcestershire sauce 63,65

Y

Yoghurt 4,76

Z

Zest 47

L

lasagna 45

Conclusion

Thank you again for downloading this book!

I hope you enjoyed reading about my book!

If you enjoyed this book, please take the time to share your thoughts and post a review on Amazon. It'd be greatly appreciated!

Write me an honest review about the book – I truly value your opinion and thoughts and I will incorporate them into my next book, which is already underway.

Thank you!

If you have any questions, **feel free to contact at:** author@sauterecipes.com

Wendy Beran

sauterecipes.com

Printed in Great Britain
by Amazon